JOHN DONNE

☞ Books in the RENAISSANCE LIVES series explore and illustrate the life histories and achievements of significant artists, intellectuals and scientists in the early modern world. They delve into literature, philosophy, the history of art, science and natural history and cover narratives of exploration, statecraft and technology.

Series Editor: François Quiviger

Already published

Artemisia Gentileschi and Feminism in Early Modern Europe
  Mary D. Garrard

Blaise Pascal: Miracles and Reason *Mary Ann Caws*

Caravaggio and the Creation of Modernity *Troy Thomas*

Giorgione's Ambiguity *Tom Nichols*

Donatello and the Dawn of Renaissance Art *A. Victor Coonin*

Hans Holbein: The Artist in a Changing World *Jeanne Nuechterlein*

Hieronymus Bosch: Visions and Nightmares *Nils Büttner*

Isaac Newton and Natural Philosophy *Niccolò Guicciardini*

John Donne: In the Shadow of Religion *Andrew Hadfield*

John Evelyn: A Life of Domesticity *John Dixon Hunt*

Leonardo da Vinci: Self, Art and Nature *François Quiviger*

Michelangelo and the Viewer in His Time *Bernadine Barnes*

Paracelsus: An Alchemical Life *Bruce T. Moran*

Petrarch: Everywhere a Wanderer *Christopher S. Celenza*

Piero della Francesca and the Invention of the Artist
  Machtelt Brüggen Israëls

Pieter Bruegel and the Idea of Human Nature *Elizabeth Alice Honig*

Raphael and the Antique *Claudia La Malfa*

Rembrandt's Holland *Larry Silver*

Rubens's Spirit: Art and Ingenuity in Early Modern Europe
  Alexander Marr

Titian's Touch: Art, Magic and Philosophy *Maria H. Loh*

Tycho Brahe and the Measure of the Heavens *John Robert Christianson*

JOHN DONNE

In the Shadow of Religion

ANDREW HADFIELD

REAKTION BOOKS

For Patrick, now striking out on his own

Published by Reaktion Books Ltd
Unit 32, Waterside
44–48 Wharf Road
London N1 7UX, UK
www.reaktionbooks.co.uk

First published 2021

Copyright © Andrew Hadfield 2021

An earlier version of parts of chapters Three and Five appeared in 'Literary Contexts: Predecessors and Contemporaries', in *The Cambridge Companion to John Donne*, ed. Achsah Guibbory (Cambridge: Cambridge University Press, 2006), pp. 49–64, © Andrew Hadfield 2006. Reprinted with permission.

Printed and bound in India by Replika Press Pvt. Ltd

A catalogue record for this book is available from the British Library

ISBN 978 1 78914 393 5

COVER: Unknown English artist, *John Donne*, c. 1595, oil on panel. © National Portrait Gallery, London

CONTENTS

Preface:
Donne the Thinker

ohn Donne (1572–1631) is a complicated poet who has had an interesting reception since his death. The revolutionary nature of his poetry was recognized almost immediately, with Thomas Pestell, a clergyman and prolific poet, calling him 'the late Copernicus in Poetrie' (1650).[1] Just as Copernicus transformed our understanding of the solar system, realizing that the earth circles the sun, so did Donne, argues Pestell, open up new possibilities for writing in English.[2]

Donne was celebrated by his first biographer, Isaak Walton (c. 1593–1683), in a publication less than a decade after Donne's death, in 1640. However, although eighteenth-century readers and writers recognized Donne's importance they felt that his rhythms and diction were too rough and harsh and sought to regularize his poetry. John Dryden (1631–1700) praised Donne's wit and ingenuity, but felt that he allowed the latter to unbalance his poetry, a judgement supported later by Samuel Johnson (1709–1784), who coined the famous term 'metaphysical poetry' after Dryden's use of the word 'metaphysics' to describe Donne's innovative poetry and use of striking, often far-fetched metaphors.[3] Alexander Pope (1688–1744)

Unknown artist, *John Donne*, 1622, oil on canvas.

paraphrased Donne's *Satires*, adapting them to eighteenth-century standards of taste, after which Donne fell largely out of favour until T. S. Eliot's famous essay revitalized interest in him. Eliot (1888–1965) argued that Donne was writing immediately before 'the disassociation of sensibility', the transformation in human understanding that severed links between art and science. In a crucial way Donne represented, to Eliot, the apex of poetic achievement in English verse:

> something . . . happened to the mind of England between the time of Donne . . . and the time of Tennyson and Browning; it is the difference between the intellectual poet and the reflective poet. Tennyson and Browning are poets, and they think; but they do not feel their thought as immediately as the odour of a rose. A thought to Donne was an experience; it modified his sensibility. When a poet's mind is perfectly equipped for its work, it is constantly amalgamating disparate experience; the ordinary man's experience is chaotic, irregular, fragmentary . . . in the mind of the poet . . . experiences are always forming new wholes.[4]

From the 1930s onwards, with the development of literary criticism as a school and university practice, and the concomitant rise of interest in English studies, Donne occupied a central place in the critical imagination in English-speaking countries, as a poet who spoke about real life in a realistic way.[5]

Donne's reputation probably reached its zenith in the 1960s, when he became the poet of (male) sexualized love, alongside D. H. Lawrence as the novelist companion, his

champions perhaps not spending as much time with his sermons or *Pseudo-Martyr* as they did with his secular poetry.[6]
Both Lawrence and Donne suffered an inevitable feminist
backlash that pointed out the problematic nature of such celebratory readings.[7] In more recent years Donne's reputation
as a popular poet has diminished somewhat, although he is
still a recognizably canonical writer who represents central
features of the English Renaissance for a wider public.[8] As
Michael Schoenfeldt has commented in a recent collection,
'Donne's seesaw reputation over the centuries offers a salutary
lesson in the shifting values of literary taste.'[9]

In the last decade there has been sustained interest in
Donne's theology and his career as dean of St Paul's and, in
particular, his sermons and theological writing, which has led
to an important re-evaluation of his reputation and a more
balanced approach to his writing and literary career.[10] This
book is part of that re-assessment of Donne's life, acknowledging also the significance of his marriage, erotic writings,
friendships and relations with patrons, and the sustained
impact of the Reformation. Donne is a major writer, his
work providing us with an insight into his times as well as
resonating well beyond them. Read as a poet of sexuality he
undoubtedly looks outdated, perhaps even offensive. Read as
a poet, theologian and writer who explores the possibilities of
the self, the body and the soul and the ability of the individual
to interact with others, as well as the limits of state power and
the nature of toleration, he looks like a significant thinker.

What this book seeks to explain is the range and diversity
of Donne's imagination and his ability – like poets whose
lives overlapped with his, Milton, Shakespeare and Spenser

– to think in poetry.[11] I am not suggesting that we go back to Eliot's now notorious analysis of the relationship between poetry and society. Rather, we need to explore Donne's work as a whole, reading the erotic lyrics, the divine poems, the controversial religious works, the satires, the verse letters, the long experimental poems, the devotions, the sermons, the proverbs, the epitaphs, the letters, if we are to appreciate how capacious and interconnected his imagination was. Of course, individual works stand alone and we would not read them if they did not have something to say to us without our having first to absorb a vast amount of contextual material and other literary works. But if we are to get beyond the familiar view of Donne as a brilliant lustful young man who turned to religion in older age when his body became subordinated to his mind, it makes sense to appreciate how he approached a variety of types, genres and kinds of writing.

Donne emerges as a writer who had a wonderful ear for English and so could coin stunning, memorable poetic phrases that appear in every book of quotations ('A bracelet of bright hair about the bone', 'for whom the *bell* tolls; It tolls for *thee*', 'Nor ever chaste, except you ravish me'). He also had an ability to push the boundaries of what was considered appropriate, which explains the frank sexuality of his love lyrics (many of which I suspect are misread because readers imagine that they must be written for a scarlet woman rather than his wife) and the apparently heretical nature of much of his religious writing. Scholars have wasted a great deal of time trying to work out the precise nature of Donne's religious belief rather than seeing him as an author who understood that thinking through complicated religious issues would inevitably run the risk of heresy.[12] This second ability would matter little if Donne could not also construct challenging arguments in both prose and verse. When put together his work stands as an extraordinary achievement, and one that has rarely been appreciated as a whole.

This book contains an overview of Donne's life and has much in common with a biography, but it is not designed to be one. My aim is to share my understanding that the more we know about Donne's life and times, the more his work will make sense and the greater the enjoyment we will take from his writing. Donne was a brilliant writer who lived through challenging times and endured complicated personal circumstances (some undoubtedly of his own making). Like many profound thinkers he seems to be a startling mixture of the ancient and the modern, so that reading him is always an unsettling experience. On the one hand, he can defend liberty of conscience, the freedom of the individual and, apparently, suicide; on the other, his poems often silence the women he claims to adore, and his arguments for a strong central authority, even absolutism, might seem conservative or reactionary.

I have divided the book into six chapters that deal with central aspects of Donne's life and his world. The first chapter explores his sense of himself and his obsession with the relationship between his body and his soul, a constant preoccupation throughout his writing career. The second examines Donne's religion and the religious context in which he was writing, as we cannot understand the work of a man who was born into a Catholic family but who died holding a position at the very centre of the English Protestant Church if we do not grapple with his omnipresent but elusive Christian faith. Chapter Three analyses some of Donne's erotic poetry, much probably written before his marriage (his poems are notoriously difficult to date with certainty). I argue that we cannot read Donne's work as the direct product of his experience, as is often assumed. Rather, his work needs also to be read in terms of a longer history of erotic poetry dating back in particular to Ovid, a tradition that enjoyed a particular vogue in late Elizabethan England. Chapter Four looks at Donne's marriage to Ann More, a relationship that defined both his life and his writing. The marriage undoubtedly brought the couple much happiness – at least, if Donne's writing serves as an accurate testimony, because we have nothing from Ann's side – but was also a disaster, limiting their circumstances and prospects.

Chapter Five deals with Donne's learning and how he used it in his writing. Donne clearly made good use of his education and was an avid book collector. He was well versed in theology and the classics, as were many of his contemporaries (although few were as assiduous readers as Donne was), and was widely read in more recent European literature. He also had far more unusual interests and enthusiasms, notably for alchemy, which features in a number of his poems, and, more significantly, pagan religious ideas, as manifested in his long poem 'Metempsychosis'. The final chapter is concerned with friendship, an especially important relationship for many in Renaissance Europe, and one that was frequently idealized. Donne in his letters and verse letters reveals that he is eager to befriend many people, both men and women. He also demonstrates that he thinks carefully about the nature of friendship, the one relationship that was predicated upon the notion that the hierarchies that stratified early modern society could be overcome by the encounter of equals who treated each other with mutual respect.

ONE

The Soul and the Self

ohn Donne is one of the few writers of the 1590s to have sat for a portrait. The painting is extremely unusual: later, portraits of writers of the 'middling sort', along with those of prominent citizens, local dignitaries, merchants and other members of local urban elites, would become relatively common, but Donne's picture is the earliest extant oil portrait of an Elizabethan poet.[1] We do not know the provenance of the painting but it seems to have hung in Lincoln's Inn, where Donne had studied, perhaps in the chambers of Donne's friend Christopher Brooke (c. 1570–1628), a politician and poet to whom Donne addressed a verse epistle and the poem 'The Storm' in the 1590s. If so, this was a work for a friend, an equal, not a superior from whom one was seeking patronage or a work designed to represent the sitter's social status and significance.

Donne sat for a number of portraits of himself throughout his life, which is, again, unusual for someone of his social status. The portraits have been seen as a means of recording his life and the transformations that he underwent (from Catholic youth, to melancholy lover, to Protestant divine, to a virtual death mask), as well as an indication of 'his habitual fascination

Unknown English artist, *John Donne*, c. 1595, oil on panel.

with his own changing identity'.[2] It is hard to disagree that Donne foregrounds himself in his work and if there is one constant feature of Donne's writing throughout his long and productive life it is his obsession with himself and his identity. But he was equally concerned with his soul and the question of whether he was to receive salvation or face damnation.[3] Therefore, a case can – and should – be made that Donne's writing career represents a sustained and complicated response to the effects of the Reformation on the individual.[4] Specifically, his work shows what happened when the individual Christian was cut off from the Church and had to make sense of the complicated, dangerous and fractious world on their own. Reformation historians used to assume that most Protestants felt that casting off the shackles of an older, repressive religious hierarchy granted the individual an exhilarating sense of liberation. Finally they could choose to worship as they wanted; could read the Bible in translation, expanding the number of believers who could understand it, and so develop new communities of Christians bound together by mutual assumptions and ideals.[5]

The reality, of course, was much less appealing. Catholics taunted Protestants with the hostile question 'Where was your Church before Luther?'[6] They argued that Protestants had no legitimacy as a coherent group, pointing out that when they had theological and religious issues Catholics had an edifice of priests, saints and the Church to guide and protect them, whereas Protestants had to rely on their unmediated relationship with God. How did they know that they were not delusional?[7] And Catholics also argued that the break-up of Christian unity would to lead to murderous conflict, with

William Marshall, after Nicholas Hilliard, 'John Donne, aged 18', engraving in John Donne, *Poems, by J. D. With Elegies on the Authors Death* (1654).

different factions of Christians insisting that they were the only righteous interpreters of God's word, a prediction that proved horribly accurate.[8]

Donne's religious poetry clearly responds to the intense pressure placed upon the individual in the aftermath of the Reformation. Holy Sonnet 9 is a logical response to such turmoil, a plea to God to extinguish him entirely:

> If pois'nous minerals, and if that tree
> Whose fruit threw death on else immortal us,
> If lecherous goats, if serpents envious
> Cannot be damned, alas, why should I be?
> Why should intent or reason, born in me,
> Make sins, else equal, in me more heinous?
> And mercy being easy and glorious
> To God, in his stern wrath why threatens he?
> But who am I, that dare dispute with thee,
> O God? Oh, of thine only worthy blood
> And my tears make a heavenly Lethean flood,
> And drown in it my sins' black memory.
> That thou remember them, some claim as debt:
> I think it mercy, if thou wilt forget.[9]

There is an obvious link between the apparently vain young man in the youthful portrait posing as a melancholy lover staring out beyond the viewer, with his conspicuously large fashionable hat, carelessly unbuttoned tunic, elegant fingers and sensuous mouth, and the apparently desperate speaker in the Holy Sonnet. After all, the speaker asks God a series of questions about why he gave mankind souls; in effect, asking

the Creator why he created people as he did.[10] The theology
may be problematic and the answers easy to provide: goats
and serpents cannot be damned because they do not have reason and souls, unlike men and women. The more significant
effect of the poem, which is hardly a theological conundrum
staged in verse, is that the speaker dares to pose these questions at all and draws attention to his bold challenge to the
Creator, asking himself and the reader who he is that risks
debating fundamental matters with God. The wish for oblivion is a further representation of the speaker's arrogance as he
lurches from challenging God to desiring to escape judgement
in any way possible, fearful that he is so exceptionally wicked
that he should be singled out for special divine treatment.

Of course, we cannot equate the speaker with Donne
himself, and should read this poem, and so many others, as a
dramatic monologue staging a particular dilemma for the
Christian, one easy to solve in logical, theological terms, but
part of common experience for Protestants after the Reformation. Would it not sometimes be easier to be destroyed, to
avoid the afterlife, than to carry on? That is surely to draw a
false conclusion and the reader will realize that Donne has
no real desire for oblivion or belief that it would be good for
others to think the same way too.

We should, I think, be sceptical of the frequently made
claims that we can separate the young lustful Jack Donne of
the erotic poems and the mature John Donne, theologian
and dean of St Paul's.[11] Not only are the poems often hard to
date, but the links between the body and theology, sex and
religion, were there from his early writings. In his secular and
his holy poems, Donne, a man from a Catholic family who

became an influential Protestant churchman, employs both Catholic and Protestant ideas and images. A particular case in point is 'The Relic', a poem in which the speaker imagines his grave dug up to make way for a more recent corpse:

> If this fall in a time, or land
> Where mis-devotion doth command,
> Then he that digs us up will bring
> Us to the bishop and the king,
>   To make us relics: then
> Thou shalt be a Mary Magdalen, and I
>   A something else thereby.
> All women shall adore us (and some men);
> And since at such time miracles are sought,
> I would have that age by this paper taught
> What miracles we harmless lovers wrought.
> (lines 12–22)

The lines are curious and challenging, caught between what might seem like idle poetic whimsy and the reality of sectarian conflict. The worship of the relics of saints was a Catholic practice condemned frequently by Protestants, one of the fundamental issues that neatly divided the branches of the faith. Protestants refused to admit the possibility of the intercession of the saints, since true Christians prayed directly to God.[12] Here the speaker imagines someone in the future – presumably a person employed by the Church who opens up the grave 'Some second guest to entertain' (line 2) – observing remnants of a skeleton with a love token: 'A bracelet of bright hair about the bone' (6). The relic, preserved in a

memorably alliterative line, is already miraculous because hair
starts to become dull immediately after death, whereas here
the lover's hair retains its sheen.[13]

The speaker refers to the future when the bones and hair
are discovered as being a time or place 'Where mis-devotion
doth command', indicating that, if this is indeed England,
Catholicism has been re-established as the state religion. The
poem takes an apparently neutral stance on a subject that can
never be imagined impartially. Is the speaker eagerly antici-
pating this prospect? The reference to the relic being brought
to the bishop and the king may be a recollection of James I's
famous episcopal injunction: 'No bishop, no king', meaning
that no Christian country could exist without a proper hierarchy and structure.[14] Assuming the poem was written after
the Hampton Court Conference (1604), when James's words
were uttered to squash the demands of the puritans for further
Church reform, does that suggest that an established Church
leads inevitably back to Rome? Or is the speaker simply
acknowledging the terrifyingly chaotic history of English religion since the Reformation, a history that deeply affected his
own family and determined the course of his life? In imagining that her hair will be taken for that of a Mary Magdalene,
famous for her luxuriant, beautiful hair, is the speaker praising
his lover's beauty, or seeing her as a racy, loose woman?[15]

As the poem was surely written after his marriage, it is
perhaps best to think of it as written for Ann Donne, like its
earlier counterpart, 'The Canonization', which defiantly celebrated his marriage, perhaps in response to criticism from
a friend about his absence from court.[16] The speaker then
assumes that, as he has been discovered next to the Magdalene,

he will be taken for something else, a man who consorts with sinners or prostitutes, indicating that their love may be misinterpreted and devalued rather than canonized. The poem can be read as a symbol of the fate of religion in hazardous, unstable times; hence the need to put the record straight and to explain the relics properly. The interpretation of relics may well divide people – as relics do – inspiring more women than men (because they are more devout or more credulous?), but when explained properly the signs of the true devotion of lovers like the Donnes should be celebrated for overcoming so many obstacles and remaining true and devout, exemplars of the properly faithful.

The poem leaves the reader in doubt about the nature of religion, and the character of Donne's own belief. It does show us how Donne did not separate the personal from the religious, the use of the self from the care of the soul, giving his writing and his faith an idiosyncratic and elusive quality.[17] Most famously he combines them in a confrontational manner in the famous Holy Sonnet 10:

> Batter my heart, three-personed God, for you
> As yet but knock, breathe, shine, and seek to mend;
> That I may rise and stand, o'erthrow me, and bend
> Your force to break, blow, burn, and make me new.
> I, like an usurped town to another due,
> Labour to admit you, but oh, to no end;
> Reason, your viceroy in me, me should defend,
> But is captived, and proves weak or untrue.
> Yet dearly I love you, and would be loved fain,
> But am betrothed unto your enemy:

Divorce me, untie or break that knot again;
Take me to you, imprison me, for I,
Except you enthral me, never shall be free,
Nor ever chaste, except you ravish me.

The poem has never ceased to shock readers in casting
God as a brutal military commander eager to imprison and,
at the end of the sonnet, rape the speaker. Given the terrifying
reality of early modern warfare, the brutal nature of sieges
after which victorious commanders would usually allow their
troops freedom to do what they wanted for a set period (especially if the town had refused to surrender), the disturbing
nature of the sonnet becomes clear.[18] Reason should function
properly to allow God's victory, but it is impeded: the true
Christian would fully surrender to God and accept whatever
the consequences were, as with those defeated in war. In the
final lines the speaker is to be divorced from Satan, breaking
the symbolic bond that unites the Christian couple, but also
suggesting that the speaker recovers the knot of their virginity through their marriage to God, alluding to the legend of
the 144,000 virgin brides of Christ (Revelation 14:1−4).[19]

The use of such dramatic and extreme imagery, combining
the erotic and the sacred, links the poem to Counter-
Reformation art and literature, which sought to emphasize
the experience of the individual Christian, the awesome
majesty of God and the ineffable nature of the sacred, in
pointed contrast to the more Protestant belief that the
Bible could and should be explained.[20] The paradox that the
poem embraces is that reason needs to be abandoned in
order for the believer to become a proper Christian, a rational

decision that acknowledges the limits of reason. Donne always characterizes religion as inextricably bound up with the self, a personal experience that can only ever be represented or understood via analogies, poetic comparisons that gesture towards the truth without fully capturing its essence. The self is inextricably related to faith, neither of which can be fully comprehended.

Donne's position is paradoxical: he puts himself on display, always aware that, in doing so, as much is hidden as is revealed. One of his late poems, 'Hymn to God, My God, in My Sickness', was written during one of the most serious of his many bouts of ill-health, from which he was likely to die. The poem may have been written on his deathbed.[21] It describes the speaker – here, Donne himself – laid out before his physicians:

> Whilst my physicians by their love are grown
>   Cosmographers, and I their map, who lie
> Flat on this bed, that by them may be shown
>   That this is my south-west discovery,
>   *Per fretum febris*, by these straits to die,
>
> I joy, that in these straits I see my West;
>   For, though their currents yield return to none,
> What shall my West hurt me? As West and East
>   In all flat maps (and I am one) are one;
>   So death doth touch the Resurrection. (6–15)

Donne imagines himself simultaneously as a map examined by the doctors seeking to cure him, and as a vessel in uncharted and dangerous waters that needs to be guided to safety (*Per fretum febris*, through the difficult course of a fever). Maps are always approximations of reality and can never be perfect representations, something of which cartographers in this period of expanding horizons and dangerous trans-oceanic voyages were acutely aware.[22] Donne foregrounds the metaphor only to allow it to slip away at the end. The flat map is an approximation of the globe, so the reality it represents is spherical, with East and West being joined together. Similarly, as he prepares for death, Donne is reminded that life does not end there because of Christ's sacrifice for mankind, which ensures that we shall all be resurrected. The sunset in the west leads to the sunrise in the east, so his physicians will either save him and he will not die (yet) or they will fail and he will die and have eternal life.

It is undoubtedly a neat poetic paradox. What the conceit also achieves, as such devices do throughout Donne's writing, is to obscure and render mysterious the nature of both the self and faith. Donne's self is stridently foregrounded here through his daring and elaborate use of metaphor to represent himself; but the nature of his experience is universalized and so made common, as all will die and be judged by God. In representing his body as a map, Donne individualizes himself from others (utilizing the language of 'my' and 'I' in the poem) while also portraying himself as an everyman, one who could represent the world at large:

Is the Pacific Sea my home? Or are
The Eastern riches? Is Jerusalem?
Anian, and Magellan, and Gibraltar,
All straits, and none but straits, are ways to them,

Whether where Japhet dwelt, or Cham, or Shem.
We think that Paradise and Calvary,
Christ's cross, and Adam's tree, stood in one place;
Look, Lord, and find both Adams met in me;
As the first Adam's sweat surrounds my face,
May the last Adam's blood my soul embrace.
(16–25)

The rhetorical questions blur the different locations into one so that they serve to connote an exoticism, incorporated as part of Donne's identity as one of God's creations. Everything becomes a strait, a narrow path that the Christian must follow to enter heaven, referencing the warning in the Bible: 'strait is the gate, and narrow is the way, which leadeth unto life, and few be that find it' (Matthew 7:14). The more dangerous the passage, just like Donne's illness, the more likely it is to lead to heaven.

The stanza ends with Donne reminded that after the Flood Noah's sons were dispersed throughout the world to form the different races that inhabit the globe. Accordingly, he becomes part of God's large human family.[23] The image draws attention to Donne's imaginative skill as a poet and to his relative insignificance. More significantly the map reveals that, like Donne's life and the history of time, man's fall and salvation are intimately connected. The sad story of a sinful life can have a happy ending.

Donne's exploration of his identity throughout his life showed that men and women are both individuals and generic types, possessing particular, specific characteristics, but ultimately needing to surrender to God's will in order to secure salvation, a paradox Donne struggled with in many of his works. Indeed, in the first of his *Paradoxes*, posthumously published as *Juvenilia* in 1633 but probably written in the early 1590s – perhaps while he was a student at Lincoln's Inn – Donne meditated on the frivolous and profound proposition 'That all things kill themselves'.[24] He argues that everything strives for perfection, which in a theocentric universe means death: 'Plants quickened and inhabited by the most unworthy Soule, which therefore neyther will, nor worke, affect an end, a perfection, a Death'. Horses, the most expertly and perfectly bred, 'will run to their own Deathes, neyther sollicited by spurs . . . nor by honor which they apprehend not' (p. 1). In similar ways men and women hasten to their deaths, inspired by virtue – the brave risk their lives more than cowards – and simply using the faculties that God has given them properly and improperly:

> we kill dayly our bodyes with Surfets, and our Minds with anguishes. Of our Powers, remembering kills our Memory. Of affections, Lusting our Lust. Of Vertues, giving kills Liberality. And if these things kill themselves, they do it in ther best and supreme perfection: for after perfection immediately followes exces: which changes the natures and the names, and makes them not the same things . . . the best things kill themselves soonest (for no perfection indures) and all things labor to this perfection, all travaile to ther owne Death. (p. 2)

The argument is specious: it is not really true to argue that only the good die young and the examples are opportunistically

chosen to challenge the reader and show off the cleverness
of the author. Lust does indeed kill lust because it has to end
(with a 'little death'), but the process can often be repeated;
remembering does not necessarily destroy the memory, and
neither does giving necessarily destroy liberality (unless, like
Timon of Athens, one gives away rather too much to those
who do not deserve it).

What Donne is exploiting, however, is the Christian tradition of life as a journey or pilgrimage that ends in death and,
one hopes, salvation. Accordingly, the crucial achievement is
to get through life without committing too many sins, or to
give oneself the chance to repent properly and expunge all
traces of vice before encountering God. The first *Paradox* does
not logically prove that things try to destroy themselves, but
it does connect to a serious, long-standing Christian tradition – as does the 'Hymn to God, My God, in My Sickness',
written much later in Donne's life – that life was something
to endure and that it should seem inconsequential when
compared to the eternity that awaited us after death.

The logic of this first *Paradox*, and Donne's thinking about
the nature of the self and the soul, is perhaps most fully analysed in Donne's most challenging and controversial work,
Biathanatos, his exploration of suicide and a work specifically
based on the notion of the paradox.[25] Like the *Paradoxes*,
Biathanatos was not published in his lifetime and first appeared
in print in 1644. Suicide was strongly condemned within the
Christian tradition as a sign of despair, the worst of all sins,
destroying the life granted to an individual by God, and
suicides could not usually be buried in hallowed ground.[26]
However, Christ's sacrifice for mankind, while celebrated by

such authorities as St Augustine, undoubtedly made the issue
more complicated for a bold and individual thinker like
Donne.[27]

Donne employs the elaborate comparisons that charac-
terize his writing to argue that the self, properly sacrificed,
not only pleases God but preserves the soul and supports
the faith:

> if in a Tempest we must cast out the most precious
> ware aboard to save the lives of the Passengers, and the
> Merchant who is damnified thereby cannot impute this
> to any, nor remedie himselfe, how much more may I,
> when I am weather-beaten, and in danger of betray-
> ing that precious soule which God hath embarqued in
> me, put off this burdenous flesh, till his pleasure be that
> I shall resume it? For this is not to sinck the ship but
> to retire it to safe harbour, and assured Anchor.[28]

The true Christian, like the passenger in a storm who realizes
that he is too feeble to survive and is therefore endangering
the lives of others, will be prepared to sacrifice himself.
Allowing the self to be destroyed for the greater good will
save the soul and enable the individual to enter heaven more
rapidly, so self-slaughter may well be the right course of
action in perilous times. Deliberately parting the soul from
the body can preserve the soul and save it from further harm.

Donne is conscious that a heavy burden is placed on those
who have to set an example to the people and persuade them
to do the right thing. He cites the example of the godly Christian who is forced by a tyrant to commit an act of idolatry

(which in Donne's lifetime meant denying and obscuring the true worship of God, a deadly sin).[29] Donne's example reveals how he thinks about the relationship between the soul and the self and that between the individual and society:

> By which Rule, if perchance a publique, exemplary person, which had a just assurance that his example would governe the people, should be forced by a Tyrant to doe an act of Idolatry, (although by circumstances he might satisfie his owne conscience that he sinned not in doing it) and so scandalize and endanger them, if the matter were so carried and disguised, that by no way he could let them know that he did it by constraint, but voluntarily, I say perchance he were better kill himself. (*Biathanatos*, p. 76)

The most significant detail here is that the public, exemplary person who commands universal respect might be able to square the idolatry with his own conscience and so be convinced that he is not really committing a sin. Donne probably has in mind the Catholic doctrines of 'equivocation' and 'mental reservation' – which were also adopted by some Protestants. These stipulated that a true believer, forced to acquiesce to hostile, ungodly authorities, could do so by articulating ambiguous statements (equivocation) or parts of a statement which they then completed silently, understanding that God would be listening (mental reservation), and so would not be guilty of lying and thus desecrating God's word. If a Christian were asked if a priest lay in their house they would be able to answer truthfully that no priest lay there, because the priest was

standing up, knowing that the questioner would take this as
a denial while God knew the real truth (equivocation). And
if a priest were asked if they were a priest they could deny
this, adding silently 'of Zeus' (that is, a pagan god) to escape
torture and death (mental reservation).[30] Donne argues to the
contrary: it is better to be executed by a tyrant than to betray
oneself out of a mistaken belief that the survival of the individual is more important than an honest espousal of the faith.
Moreover, such quibbling dishonesty and spurious satisfying
of the individual conscience may well, it is implied, imperil
the individual's soul.

In *Biathanatos* Donne is acutely aware of the paradoxical
nature of his argument. We both possess ourselves and we do
not, because what we have has been granted to us by God and
we need to glorify him:

> Our body is so much our owne, as we may use it to
> Gods glory; and it is so little our owne, as when hee is
> pleased to have it, we doe well in resigning it to him
> by what Officer soever he accept it, whether by Angell,
> Sicknesse, Persecution, Magistrate, or our selves. (p. 78)

The argument is related to the more traditional notion that
despair is the worst sin: that our bodies and selves are never
simply our own but belong to the God who made them.[31]
Donne accepts the same premises, but includes the possibility
that self-sacrifice might be added if the individual is convinced
that it is part of God's plan, rather than a desperate denial of
God's gift to mankind. Suicide, far from being a divine injunction, is restricted and prohibited, not unreasonably, by human

law and custom. Even so, we need to remember that 'our maine periods, of Birth, of Death, and of chief alterations in this life be more immediately wrought upon by Gods determination' (p. 83). If suicide is part of God's plan for us, then it is a road that has to be taken. We need to act, as far as we can determine, in accordance with his wishes.

Donne's most profound meditation on the nature of his soul is surely his great sermon on his own imminent death, *Deaths Duell, Or, A Consolation to the Soule, against the Dying Life, and Living Death of the Body*.[32] The sermon was preached by the mortally ill Donne – in the presence of Charles I at Whitehall on 25 February 1631 – on Psalm 68, verse 20: 'And unto the lord belong the issues of death'. Donne died on 31 March and the sermon was published a year later with a portrait by Martin Droeshout the younger (1601–1650?), who had earlier produced the portrait of Shakespeare for the first folio of his *Works* (1623). The image is based on Donne in his shroud, as is the funeral monument, and the published sermon is followed by two elegies, one probably written by Donne's friend the bishop and poet, Henry King (1592–1669), the other perhaps by Edward Hyde (1607–1659).[33] King's poem celebrates Donne's achievements in lines reminiscent of his metaphysical style, as he asserts that Donne will live on after his death:

> Or els that awfull fire, which once did burne
> In thy cleare braine, now fal'ne into thy urne,
> Lives there to fright rude Empericks [physicians]
>   from thence,
> Which might profane thee by their ignorance.[34]

Martin Droeshout,
'John Donne in a
Winding Sheet',
engraving in John
Donne, *Deaths Duell*
(1632).

It is a fitting tribute, both as a striking image of the fiery thoughts of Donne continuing to burn in the funeral urn and as a recognition of Donne's writing throughout his life on the inviolable nature of the soul. Furthermore, in concentrating on Donne as a life force thriving after death it stands as both a contrast to the sermon's subject and a confirmation of its ultimate message: that through Christ we live on.

Donne's sermon serves as an extraordinary public testimony to his life and provides his final thoughts on the state of his soul as he prepares for death. Donne acknowledges that death is God's prerogative, part of his design for the world:

William Sedgwick, *Monument to John Donne*, 1640 drawing of the 1631 marble sculpture by Nicholas Stone in St Paul's Cathedral, London.

'unto this *God the Lord belong the issues of death*' (emphasis in original and in subsequent quotations from sermons) (p. 231) is quibbling on the term 'issue' meaning birth, linking the end and the beginning of life ('I am the Alpha and the Omega, the first and the last, the beginning and the end': Revelation 22:13). The union of spirit and flesh that God achieved and experienced when his son sacrificed himself to save mankind as Jesus Christ is built into the cycle of life and experienced by everyone:

> Our very *birth* and entrance into this life, is *exitus à morte*,[35] an *issue from death*, for in our mothers *wombe* wee are *dead so*, as that wee doe *not know* wee *live*, not so much as wee doe in our *sleepe*, neither is there any *grave* so close, or so *putrid* a *prison*, as the *wombe* would be unto us, if we stayed in it *beyond* our time, or dyed there *before* our time. (p. 232)

Everything that determines and surrounds our life reminds us how close we are to dying once we are born so that, in the words of *The Book of Common Prayer*, 'in the midst of life we are in death.'[36]

The proximity of death is not something to be feared, according to Donne, but to be embraced: as our souls have always belonged to God so should we want them to return to him. Donne quotes Jeremiah 1:5 to make his point: 'Before *I formed thee I knew thee*, and *before thou camest out of the wombe I sanctified thee*' (p. 233). The more we accept the omnipresence of death, the better we will understand life:

wee have a winding sheete in our Mothers wombe,
which growes with us from our conception, and wee
come into the world, wound up in that *winding sheet*, for
wee come to *seeke a grave*; And as prisoners discharg'd
of actions may lye for fees; so when the *wombe* hath
discharg'd us, yet we are bound to it by *cordes of flesh* by
such a *string*, as that wee cannot goe thence, nor stay
there; wee celebrate our owne funerals with cryes, even
at our birth; as though our *threescore and ten years life* were
spent in our mothers labour, and our circle made up
in the first point thereof. (pp. 233–4)

Donne equates the placenta and the winding sheet as
memento mori, exploring further the relationship between
death and life, the beginning and the end, which is reiterated throughout the Bible and the litany of the Church of
England in *The Book of Common Prayer*, and a preoccupation in
poems of his such as 'Hymn to God, My God, in My Sickness'.
Life, like the ends of the earth represented in that poem, is a
circle. The most significant words in this passage are 'wee
come to *seeke a grave*', the belief that life is time to be endured
rather than enjoyed and that the sooner we can cast off our
mortal flesh the happier we will be. For Donne we are imitations of Christ, reluctantly experiencing the suffering of
life knowing that our proper reward will be in heaven. Life
on earth is a gestation period preparing us for everlasting
heavenly bliss.

   Donne argues that the union of Christ's body and the soul
is a '*hypostaticall union* of both *natures*' (p. 236), the fundamental
joining of different substances, and one that meant that God

had to experience the pains of death. This mysterious union is therefore present in everyone as we all have bodies as well as souls, something that we may not be able to understand but should accept as a fundamental tenet of God's grace: 'wee looke no further for *causes* or *reasons* in the *mysteries of religion*, but to the *will* and pleasure of *God*' (p. 236). Christ rose again without experiencing the corruption of death; we will only have to suffer the pains of death for a tiny period of time before we are resurrected and united with God:

> *we shall not all sleepe* [that is, not continue in the state
> of the dead in the grave], *but wee shall all be changed in an*
> *instant*, we shall have a *dissolution*, and in the *same instant*
> a *redintegration*, [joining together again] a *recompacting* of
> *body* and *soule*, and that shall be truely a death & truely
> a resurrection. (pp. 237–8)

Donne's imagery suggests that he has in mind the rising of the bodies out of the graves on the Day of Judgement, which has led some commentators to argue that he was a 'mortalist': one who believed that the body died with the soul to sleep until it rose up to heaven at the end of time, therefore avoiding the separation of the body and the soul.[37] But, given Donne's desire to experiment with complicated and difficult ideas, and his use of elaborate comparisons and metaphors, we do not need to interpret his apparent theological position in such a literal manner. Furthermore, he warns us that we cannot and should not try to understand all the intricacies of the faith and to know more than is humanly possible:

The humble soule (and onely the humble soule is the
religious soule) rests upon *Gods* purposes, and his decrees
... the *Mysteries* of our *Religion*, are *not* the *objects* of
our reason, but *by faith we rest* on *Gods decree* and purpose.
(pp. 236–7)

The sermon contains, it is implied, helpful explanations for
the congregation, practical instruction about how to live and
not decrees and propositions explaining the nature of God.
Donne applies the message of his sermon to himself: 'I thank
him that *prayes* for me when the *Bell* tolles, but I thank him
much more that *Catechises* mee, [instructs me in religion] or

Maerten de Vos, *The Last Judgement*, 1570, oil on panel.

preaches to mee, or *instructs mee how to live*' (p. 240). Until the moment of death it was important to know how to live well. It is worth noting, however, that while Donne asks for Christian instruction he does not state what sort of education he requires, carefully eliding religious divisions.

Donne's final sermon helps us make sense of much earlier works such as Divine Meditation II, 'Death! be not proud':

Death! be not proud, though some have called thee
Mighty and dreadful, for thou art not so;
For those whom thou think'st thou dost overthrow
Die not, poor Death, nor yet canst thou kill me.
From rest and sleep, which but thy pictures be,
Much pleasure, then from thee much more must flow,
And soonest our best men with thee do go,
Rest of their bones, and soul's delivery.
Thou'rt slave to fate, chance, kings, and desp'rate men,

Unknown artist, *Doom Painting*, c. 1170, mural depicting images of the ways of salvation and damnation and their result, Church of St Peter and St Paul, Chaldon.

And dost with poison, war, and sickness dwell;
And poppy or charms can make us sleep as well
And easier than thy stroke; why swell'st thou then?
One short sleep past, we wake eternally,
And death shall be no more: Death, thou shalt die
(*Complete Poems*, pp. 541–2)

The poem only really makes sense if read in terms of Donne's thinking about the relationship between the body and the soul and the transitory nature of life. Death, so often represented as a ferocious figure, as in Hans Holbein's woodcut of Death taking the life of an emperor, is here rendered feeble and servile. Death imagines that he is a powerful warrior defeating all who cross his path, killing as and when he pleases. His servants are represented in the traditional Christian image of the Four Horsemen of the Apocalypse, wreaking havoc as the final days approach.[38] In Donne's sonnet he is mankind's lowly servant – a slave – easing the path of virtuous men and women to paradise. Death does not determine events, causing catastrophes and spreading panic; rather, he is subject to the whims of fate and fortune, dependent on the actions of men and women whose behaviour controls what he is able to achieve.

Donne's poem shows that Death has become a subordinate figure because what he grants is desirable and not, as has been assumed and is believed by the figure Donne addresses, to be feared. Donne's representation of Death can be contrasted to that of George Herbert (1593–1633), also revising the tradition that saw him as the grim reaper:

Hans Lützelburger after Hans Holbein the Younger, *Dance of Death: The Emperor*, c. 1524–6, woodcut.

Death, thou wast once an uncouth hideous thing,
    Nothing but bones,
      The sad effect of sadder groans:
Thy mouth was open, but thou couldst not sing.

For we consider'd thee as at some six
    Or ten years hence,
      After the losse of life and sense,
Flesh being turn'd to dust, and bones to sticks.
(1–8)[39]

Herbert's Death is a handsome, popular and gregarious figure:

But since our Saviour's death did put some blood
    Into thy face,
      Thou art grown fair and full of grace,
Much in request, much sought for, as a good.

For we do now behold thee gay and glad,
    As at dooms-day;
      When souls shall wear their new array,
And all thy bones with beauty shall be clad. (13–20)

As in Donne's poem, people can look forward to the Day of Judgement knowing they will be saved, secure in God's grace.

    The poems have similar premises and share a common ground but in other ways there is a stark contrast that highlights what Donne achieves in his sonnet. Herbert imagines an easy transition from life to death, one that is assisted, benign and sought out by the true Christian (Herbert does not write about suicide but his poetry does not condemn those who seek a voluntary death). Donne's poem is more confrontational, casting Death as a proud, cowardly enemy who has to be overcome and to realize that he is a servant and not a master. The poem contains the grim, traditional imagery associated with death – poison, war and sickness caused by fate, chance, power and malice. But here it is Death who must be defeated and die. For Donne, there is pleasure to be had from thinking about the figure of Death but it is the enjoyment of a triumph, a victory over a proud foe after a long struggle that has finally re-established the proper order of things, and enables men and women to look forward to the pleasures of the afterlife.

Donne's victory over Death, as in Herbert's poem, unites body and soul to create an undivided self. Death, after Christ's intervention to save mankind, becomes a liberating figure, facilitating the fusion of the elements that constitute the self when the painful pilgrimage of life ends: 'whilest wee are *in the body*, wee are but in *a pilgrimage*, and wee are *absent from the Lord*' (*Deaths Duell*, p. 234). Death dies because he actually causes life to happen after death so that all his violent aggression serves only to further God's plans to mankind's advantage. The body and the soul are combined as one self when we die and become who we really are. These paradoxes – when we die we really live; we can only inhabit our proper bodies when our earthly ones expire; we only become free and truly ourselves when we surrender to God – are central to Donne's writing and thinking throughout his life.[40] After all, he wrote the *Paradoxes* in the early 1590s while still a young man. The balance of his thought clearly changed as he grew older, and like many people, he may have regretted things he said and did when young. Even so, it is surely time to abandon the popular myth of John Donne the lecherous young man about town and the pious aged Dr Donne, dean of St Paul's.

The Reformation shaped how Donne lived and thought and left him isolated from a Church in which he could feel at home and continue the tradition of worship practised by his family. We often discuss Donne's religion in terms of Protestantism and Catholicism, but this may be to miss a more fundamental point. Like many, perhaps most, English people in a post-Schism world he had to rely on himself and his personal relationship with God to determine how he should live in the world. The Reformation may or may not have thrown his early beliefs into doubt, but the concentration on the relationship between the self and the soul remained with him throughout his relatively long life, a constant preoccupation in the interesting times in which he lived.

TWO

Religion

ohn Donne was born into a prominent Catholic family in London between January and June 1572, the third of six children. His father, John (*c.* 1535–1576), was a successful merchant and warden of the Ironmongers' Company; his mother, Elizabeth Heywood (*c.* 1543–1631), was the youngest daughter of John Heywood (1496/7–*c.* 1578), playwright, epigrammatist and loyal supporter of Mary Tudor in Henry VIII's last years, which saw him indicted for treason. John Heywood had married Joan Rastell, daughter of John Rastell and Elizabeth, the sister of saint and martyr Sir Thomas More (1478–1535). Two of Elizabeth Heywood's siblings, John Donne junior's uncles, Ellis Heywood (1529–1578) and Jasper Heywood (1535–1598), had successful academic careers at Oxford before becoming Jesuits in exile. (The Jesuits, an order founded in 1540, were followers of St Ignatius Loyola (1491–1556), committed to converting Protestants and the heathen through sending missions, and were particularly feared in England). Jasper was also well known as a dramatist and translator of Seneca and he led the Jesuit mission to England (1581–3), where he was captured, imprisoned and sentenced to death but exiled

instead (he died in Naples). Like her brothers, Elizabeth was well known as a devout Catholic. As David Colclough has commented, 'Through his connection with the More and the Heywood families Donne was thus associated with many men and women who had remained true to the Roman Catholic faith and suffered as a result.'[1] Donne inherited a long-standing Catholic tradition and his family was to make much of their connection to Sir Thomas More, Donne's great-great-uncle.[2]

Donne's father died in 1576 and his mother remarried: first, Dr John Syminges, a notable medical doctor who had

Francisco de Zurbarán, *St Ignatius Loyola*, c. 1634–50, oil on canvas.

been president of the Royal College of Physicians on several occasions; then, after Syminges died in 1588, she married – around 1590 – Richard Rainsford, another prominent Catholic. Donne matriculated at Hart Hall (now Hertford College), Oxford, in October 1584, starting his university career very young (twelve); this was probably to avoid having to swear to the queen's supremacy as Head of the Church and to the Thirty-nine Articles, the religious doctrines that had been established for the Elizabethan Church in 1571 (an oath that all adults could be required to swear).[3] He left without taking a degree (as did most Catholics who refused to swear oaths of loyalty to the Church of England). His whereabouts in the next few years are uncertain, but it is most likely that he travelled in Europe and had contact with Catholics in Europe.[4] He was admitted to Lincoln's Inn in May 1592; his brother Henry, who had studied at Oxford alongside him, was presumably studying there too. In early May 1593 a priest, William Harrington, was discovered in Henry's chambers and the two young men were arrested. Harrington denied he was a priest but Henry admitted under cross-examination that Harrington was and that he had been blessed by him. Harrington was hanged, drawn and quartered at Tyburn on 18 February 1594, and Henry Donne died of the plague in prison.[5] The episode has been seen as crucial in the development of Donne's thinking, not least by John Carey, who argues that Donne consciously abandoned his faith and become an apostate, something which haunted him for the rest of his life: 'there can be no mistake about the agony of Donne's choice. And he chose hell.'[6] According to Carey, Donne was so terrified by his brother's awful fate that he abandoned what he always believed to be the true religion.

Whatever the reason for the choice he made, it certainly helped Donne's worldly success, and he appears to have been interested in pursuing a career at court or in public life from his youth.[7] He was able to employ a servant in 1595, a sign that he must have been relatively prosperous. In 1596 he sailed as an adventurer on the expedition led by Robert Devereux, 2nd Earl of Essex, and Sir Walter Raleigh to capture Cadiz, where he wrote 'The Storm', followed by another voyage to the Azores, during which he wrote another voyage poem, 'The Calm'. Afterwards he was employed in the service of the powerful Sir Thomas Egerton (1540–1617), one of the principal lawyers of Elizabethan and Jacobean England. He entered Parliament as MP for Brackley in 1601, and a successful career as a courtier was clearly waiting for him.

However, in December 1601 he secretly married Ann More, the sixteen- or seventeen-year-old daughter of Sir George More, Egerton's brother-in-law. He subsequently informed his father-in-law but was dismissed from his post and imprisoned in the Fleet Prison before his marriage was declared lawful by the Court of Audiences (an ecclesiastical court held by the Archbishop of Canterbury in Lambeth Palace).[8] Donne's hopes of advancement at court were over and, although his father-in-law had to accept the legality of the marriage, he refused to support his daughter and seems to have blocked – or made it clear that he would be displeased by – any attempt to advance his son-in-law's prospects. Donne spent much of the next fifteen years living in a number of lodgings, dependent on the support of friends; desperately seeking stable employment with little success; writing poetry; and fathering children.[9] He did, however, build up a large circle of friends and patrons, writing letters and dedicating poems to many.

He was indeed prolific in the period 1609–15, making use of his vast learning in canon and civil law and theology in both his prose and poetry. He wrote *Biathanatos* (*c.* 1607–8), then turned to his most substantial and probably significant prose work, *Pseudo-Martyr*, published in 1610, a controversial treatise that looks as though it was designed to reach a wide audience and was surely meant to ingratiate him with the king, but which also reflected his serious thinking about loyalty to Church and state.[10] He then completed a satirical attack on Catholicism and, in particular, the Jesuits. *Ignatius His Conclave*, published in 1611, indicates that Donne, whatever he believed, was prepared to be loyal to the state in public.[11]

Donne had been advised by friends that he should consider a career in the Church. He made a final series of attempts to secure public employment: he was returned as MP for Taunton in 1614; petitioned to be made ambassador to Venice; and wrote directly to King James asking for employment. When it became clear that none of these pleas would be successful he finally acquiesced and decided to enter the Church; whether through conviction or convenience has long been debated. Donne was ordained deacon and priest at St Paul's Cathedral on 23 January 1615 and appointed a royal chaplain, required to preach before the monarch on occasion. He was given a number of other ecclesiastical livings in Kent and Huntingdon and, for the rest of his life, he would preach in various parish churches and at Court, Lincoln's Inn and

John Gipkyn, *Old St Paul's*, diptych, 1616, detail of the inside left panel showing public preaching at St Paul's in the presence of the king and his civic officials.

St Paul's Cathedral. Ann Donne died after giving birth to
a still-born child in August 1617. In 1621, when the incum-
bent, Valentine Cary, was made bishop of Exeter, Donne was
made dean of St Paul's, the head of the chapter of the cathedral, its governing body, a position he held until his death in
1631. Donne's sermons were widely celebrated and he clearly
impressed the king, who ensured that many were printed in
Donne's lifetime. After several bouts of serious illness – and
rumours of his death – Donne realized that his health could
not recover, made his will and prepared for death, preaching
his last sermon, *Deaths Duell*, a month before he died on 31
March 1631.[12]

The exact nature of Donne's religious belief and confessional allegiance is hard to determine. This mystery should
not be surprising given the complicated nature of the times
in which he lived and the tortuous nature of his family history.[13] Was Donne always really a Catholic in spirit who had
to become a Protestant to disguise his true faith? Or did he
turn against the tradition of Catholic opposition to the state
Church and seek to make his compromise with it? Until the
publication of Pope Pius v's papal bull in 1570, declaring
that Elizabeth was a heretic queen whom Catholics loyal to
the papacy should seek to overthrow in order to re-establish
the true faith, many Catholics had reluctantly accepted the
status quo and often practised their religion in private. After
that pivotal moment, and the subsequent Jesuit missions of
the late 1570s and early 1580s, the hostility of the Protestant
authorities to Catholics split the Catholic community into
those loyal to the state ('Appellants') and those who supported the Pope.[14] For some commentators, Donne's careful

evasion of any commitment, his ambiguous and slippery theological language, and his apparent adoption of possibly heretical positions (for example, mortalism) suggest that he may even have belonged to a sect condemned by both Churches.[15]

A more fruitful way of exploring Donne's religious belief may be to turn away from thinking about his adherence to a particular confessional allegiance and to understand his religion in terms of loyalty to an institution (as well as a bold desire to imagine different religious positions). Many scholars have started to recognize that simply imagining the Reformation as a battle between two conflicting loyalties and faiths does not do justice to the complicated nature of religious disputes in the period. People did not simply choose one set of beliefs over another: for example, whether they thought the Church had the authority to interpret the Bible or the individual Christian had the right to choose themselves; whether the sacraments literally changed into the blood and body of Christ when blessed by the priest (transubstantiation) or the change was primarily symbolic (consubstantiation); or whether the mass should be in Latin or English. Of course, such issues mattered to most people, but they may not have been the only considerations persuading people how to act and behave. Many, probably including Donne, who had witnessed the consequences at first hand, would have been afraid of the terrifying instruments of state persecution and the appalling punishments meted out to those who fell foul of the law.[16] Resisting had severe consequences. Furthermore, there was the confusion and misery of witnessing a Church that had managed to stay unified for

one and a half millennia being finally torn apart and dividing
communities that had held together until then. Along with
this split came the obvious fear — what did it mean not to
have a Church in which to worship together? What were the
consequences of divided worship and were these worse than
staying together in one Church even if Christians did not
agree on everything?

Many historians now think that the majority of English
Christians after the Reformation, probably more Catholic
than Protestant in inclination, can be classified as 'Church
papists': Christians who were traditional in their belief and
were inclined to tolerate the status quo rather than cause
further schism, or who felt that it was their acceptance of the
status quo that would keep the Catholic faith alive.[17] *Pseudo-
Martyr* provides an intellectual framework for supporting the
established Church whatever the inclination or exact belief
of the individual.[18] The work justifies those who wished to
remain as 'Church papists' rather than opposing the institution as part of a concerted crusade. Donne's treatise was
written in the wake of the Gunpowder Plot (5 November
1605), an act aimed at ending the ecumenical first years of
James's reign and either overthrow him or force him to under-
take more repressive measures and so make English Catholics
take sides.[19] The immediate result was the passing of the Oath
of Allegiance, which forced subjects to swear loyalty to the
king and condemn the claims of the Pope when the authorities requested. The loyal subject had to acknowledge James
as the 'lawful and rightful King of this realm' and publicly
declare that the Pope had no power to depose the king or to
'discharge any of his Subjects of their allegiance and obedience

to his Majesty', a confrontational formula designed to make Catholics choose whether to be loyal subjects of the crown or the Church.[20]

Pseudo-Martyr is a sustained defence of the monarchy, but it is anything but a secular work. Donne argues that the monarch needs to have an authority that cannot be challenged and which is outside religious debate, a means of ensuring the liberty of James's subjects to practise their faith in private as long as they do not disturb the secular power of the state. In many ways it is a counterpart to James's *The Trew Law of Free Monarchies* (1598), which argued that, as the king's power derived from God, he should be left alone to govern as he saw fit – the best way to ensure that he governed as fairly as he could because he was answerable to God – and that his subjects were free to pursue their interests protected by a stable crown.[21] It is possible that James's writings, notably *Triplici nodo* (1607), James's defence of the Oath of Allegiance, 'inspired Donne to write *Pseudo-Martyr*'.[22]

Donne argues that 'all power is from God' (p. 79), but he is clear that this is secular authority, a central power that devolves government to the magistrates to run the country. While the basis of kingly authority is godly, the reality of monarchical rule is not: 'Nor is secular authority so *mediate*, or dependent upon men, as that it may at any time be extinguished, but must ever reside in some forme or other' (p. 78). For Donne, secular authority cannot and should not be challenged, because to do so is to undermine religious freedom, a direct challenge to James's Catholic opponents such as Robert Parsons, who claimed that all secular figures and institutions were answerable to the Church.[23]

The fear that monarchs would once again become over-
mighty, assume titles that gave them religious as well as
secular authority, start to insist on conformity and even
persecute their subjects in the name of religious unity, is
omnipresent throughout *Pseudo-Martyr*:

> All this I say, not to encourage princes to returne to
> those styles, which Christian humilitie hath made
> them dis-accustome, and leave off, and which could not
> be reassum'd without much scandal, but to shew the
> iniquitie and perversenesse of those men, who think
> great Titles belong to Kings, not as Kings, but as
> Papisticall Kings. (p. 56)

Donne argues that the Oath of Allegiance counteracts such
fears and he praises this far-sighted policy as an obvious,
practical solution for all James's subjects, providing them
with the religious freedom they require:

> If therefore the matter of this oath be so evident, as
> being Morall, & therefore constant and ever the same,
> that it can never neede his judgement, because it can
> in no case be sinne, the scruple which some have had,
> that by denying this power absolving, his spiritual
> power is endamaged, is vaine and frivolous. (p. 254)

The Oath, according to Donne, is simply sensible policy pre-
cisely because it involves no need to think and cannot envelop
the swearer in sin, leaving Christians free to employ their
spiritual and intellectual energies more fruitfully elsewhere.

Therefore, it liberates men and women to act as their conscience sees fit, enabling them to choose the religious path that seems right to them without threatening the authority of the ruler. Oaths, binding agreements that commit the swearer to follow or avoid courses of action, are vital to the functioning of Christian society but they must not be abused either by the authorities or the oath-taker.[24]

Donne acknowledges the need for oaths and makes a telling contrast between the false oaths imposed by the Catholic Church and the necessary oath undertaken by the loyal subject of the British king:

> And at no time, and to no persons, can such *Oathes* be more necessary, then to us now, who have been awakened with such drummes as these, *There is no warre in the world so just and honourable, be it civill or forraigne, as that which is waged for the Romane Religion.* And especially in this consideration are *Oathes* a fit and proper wall and Rampart, to oppose against these men, because they say, *That to the obedience of this Romane Religion, all Princes and people have yielded themselves, either by Oath, vow, or Sacraments, or every one of them.* For against this their imaginary oath, it is best, that a true, reall, and lawfull oath be administered by us. (p. 242)

Donne draws a pointed contrast between the true and proper Oath of Allegiance, and the false and deluded oath of absolute loyalty demanded by the Pope and the Catholic Church. In fact, the oath demanded by the legitimate secular authority is a reaction to the wicked and destructive promise extorted

by the Pope to fulfil his deluded claims to hegemony over
kings and their subjects. The Oath of Allegiance is the very
opposite of a tyrannical policy; rather it is a vital form of
protection against claims that will encourage religious persecution and so undermine the balance between religious
and secular life. Only foolish and unnatural thinking will
confuse and conflate these two forms of authority:

> Nor is there any thing more monstrous, and unnaturall
> and disproportioned, then that *spirituall* power should
> conceive or beget *temporall*: or to rise downwards, as
> the more degrees of height, and Supremacie, and per-
> fection it hath, the more it should decline and stoope
> to the consideration of secular and temporall matters.
> (p. 250)

Donne again shows his delight in paradox: the more religion
concerns itself with secular matters and claims supremacy
over political powers, the less spiritual it becomes, sully-
ing and diluting the sacred and undermining the legitimate
authority of the prince. For Donne the crucial point is that
we should all be responsible for our own souls and salvation,
if permitted by earthly institutions and if the authorities do
not mislead us or force us to act against God's will:

> when all things are in such sort wel composed and
> established, and every subordinate Wheele set in
> good order, we are guilty of our owne damnation, if
> wee obey not the Minister, and the Minister is guilty
> of it, if hee neglect to instruct us, so is the Prince

> guilty of our spiritual ruine, and eternall perishing, if
> hee doe not both provide able men to give us spirit-
> uall foode, and punish both their negligence and our
> transgressions. (p. 144)

The penalties for confusing the spiritual and the secular
are catastrophic. Not only is proper rule compromised and
realms placed in unnecessary danger, but everyone concerned
is in grave danger of eternal damnation.

Such passages remind us of the central point of *Pseudo-
Martyr*: that death in the service of illegitimate authority is
not merely futile, but diabolical, likely to imperil the soul of
the victim rather than elevate him or her to heavenly bliss.
It is the duty of authorities to facilitate the salvation of the
subjects entrusted to their care, something best achieved by
leaving them alone to make their own decisions rather than
coercing them and so removing the power of choice. *Pseudo-
Martyr* is central to our understanding of Donne's intellectual
and religious beliefs during James's reign. It explains his loyal
adherence to the monarch as well as his decision to pursue a
career in the Church of England.[25] Donne had lived under the
threat of imprisonment and possible execution throughout
his life, but the Oath of Allegiance provided a means of providing safety and squaring conscience (although it is worth
noting that he never seems to have been in danger of being
asked to take it).

Donne's public arguments about religion are concerned
with combatting not only tyranny, but the imposition of a
unified belief and the coercion of individuals to expose their
allegiance. It is hardly surprising, therefore, that his poetry

and sermons should explore the mysteries of the Christian faith without revealing obvious clues of the nature of the author's own belief.[26] Indeed, many of Donne's poems adopt a startled conditional style, as if he were suddenly surprised by the nature of the faith he knows he has to accept but has yet to understand. A case in point is Holy Sonnet 4:

> At the round earth's imagined corners, blow
> Your trumpets, angels! and arise, arise
> From death, you numberless infinities
> Of souls, and to your scattered bodies go!
> All whom the Flood did and fire shall o'erthrow,
> All whom war, dearth, age, agues, tyrannies,
> Despair, law, chance hath slain, and you whose eyes
> Shall behold God, and never taste death's woe.
> But let them sleep, Lord, and me mourn a space,
> For if above all these my sins abound,
> 'Tis late to ask abundance of thy grace
> When we are there; here on this lowly ground
> Teach me how to repent; for that's as good
> As if thou'dst seal'd my pardon with thy blood.

As in *Deaths Duell*, Donne refers to the widespread belief that the Apocalypse was imminent.[27] The angels will blow their trumpets after the breaking of the last seal, there being seven seals that secure the secret book or scroll that appears to John of Patmos in his vision. Once they are broken (Revelation 5–8), the Apocalypse starts, the four horsemen riding out after the breaking of the fourth seal (6:1–8); the fifth seal releasing the cries of martyrs demanding the wrath of God be visited upon wicked mankind (6:9–11); the sixth seal causing natural disasters (6:12–17); and the seventh producing the angels who blow their trumpets (8–11), heralding the entry of the Whore of Babylon riding on a dragon as the world moves towards the final battle between Christ and Satan.

Donne's magnificent sonnet attempts to give some sense of the terror of this moment, which is surely beyond comprehension. The poem opens with the impossible notion of 'imagined corners' of the globe, an image that derives from Donne's interest in scientific developments and map making (he probably has in mind the common images of cherubs or other mythological figures blowing winds in the corners of maps).[28] Just as his diseased body was conceived as a map in which the edges could be joined to produce the three-dimensional space that a two-dimensional map represents in 'Hymn to God, My God, in My Sickness', so now the three-dimensional globe is imagined as a map with corners.[29] The poem alerts the reader to the fact that they will need to think in stranger and more challenging ways than they have ever imagined if they are even to begin to understand the nature of the Apocalypse. In doing so he is recasting the disturbing nature of the final book of the Bible in order to capture its powerful effect and point readers towards the significance of its message. The final couplet is as challenging as the opening image, so that the substance of the sonnet is enveloped in startling thoughts. Just as the first line asks the reader to imagine something impossible, so does the last couplet describe Christ's mercy as though it were hypothetical rather than, as Donne of course thinks, a given. If the speaker is taught how to repent, then that is as good as Christ sacrificing himself for mankind. The shock is that, of course, this is what has happened, so the speaker, apparently ignorant of the faith, can be saved.

Donne's Holy Sonnets have been read as works influenced by Calvin's doctrine of 'double predestination', the belief that God both knows and pre-ordains the future so that the saved and the damned have already been judged before they are born.[30] But it is not necessary to narrow them down to one particular religious position. Rather, as with 'The Relic', which toys with a particularly Catholic practice, they experiment with different religious positions. Holy Sonnet 4 imagines a despairing Christian unable to understand how God can ever forgive him for his manifold sins, thinking about the most terrifying and awful aspect of Christian theology, and finding that, in fact, he does start to understand the nature of God's grace. The paradoxical nature of Donne's thinking is obvious once again. The octave of the sonnet describes the impending Apocalypse and bodies rising out of their graves to be clothed once again with flesh, a scene that would have been depicted in many English churches before they were white-washed after the Reformation, and which Donne would have seen on his European travels.[31] It concludes with a direct address to those who will not die because they will be taken to heaven when the world ends, which may, of course, include the reader, demonstrating an urgent sense that the world was about to end. The sonnet changes dramatically in the sestet, with the speaker desperate to slow down time, pleading with God that He forget his sins as he fears that he is too late to save himself from eternal damnation. The piece becomes more introspective as the speaker asks God to show him how

he might repent before we move to the final twist and we realize that he can repent, and may actually have done so in the poem.

This sonnet does not obviously represent the thoughts of a despairing poet; neither is it particularly Calvinist in style, tone or content. Nor is it a work that we have to take at face value as a statement of the poet's faith and it tells us very little about what Donne might have believed. The fear that the Apocalypse could happen at any time was common to both Protestants and Catholics, as was the belief that salvation depended on Christ's sacrifice. Where the poem might be more unusual is in the confused, terrified and despairing voice of the speaker, reminiscent of that of many psalms, a mode of address frequently adopted in Donne's sermons and poems. Psalms were translated and imitated much more frequently after the Reformation than they were in the centuries immediately before, in particular by Protestants trying to articulate their sense of isolation and need for God's guidance in spiritually troubled times. Donne's speaker sounds exactly like the voice in many penitential psalms, most obviously that in Psalm 51, also called the *Miserere*.[32] The Sternhold and Hopkins translation, the one most frequently used in English churches from 1562 to 1696, begins:

> Lord, consider my distresse,
> and now with speede some pitie take;
> My sins deface, my faults redress,
> good Lord, for thy great mercies sake.
> Washe me (O Lord), and make me cleane
> from this unjust and sinfull acte:

Detail of Luca Signorelli, *The Resurrection of the Flesh*, c. 1500, fresco.

And purifie yet once againe
My haynous crime and bloody fact.

Remorse and sorrowe do constrayne
me to acknowledge my excesse:
My sinne alas doth still remayne
before my face without release.
For thee alone have I offended,
committyng evill in thy sight:
And if I were therefore condemned,
yet were thy judgments just and right.[33]

The psalmist acknowledges his faults and knows that he cannot hope to win back God's favour, just as Donne's speaker does. He asks God to erase his sins and to be somehow made clean again, knowing that he holds no cards and his only recourse is to beg for mercy. The psalm ends with the psalmist hoping that God will accept his repentance and be merciful rather than exercise true judgement:

Lord unto Sion turne thy face,
poure out thy mercies on thy hill:
And on Jerusalem thy grace,
build up the walles and love it still.

Thou shalt accept then our offringes,
of peace righteousnesse I say:
Yea Calves and many other thinges,
upon thine altar will we lay. (p. 150)

Donne's Holy Sonnet 4 might be read as a meditation on
the *Miserere* against the background of catastrophic change.
The speaker is unsure of his salvation but the reader understands from what his despairing voice articulates that it is
within his grasp if he seizes his chance. Accordingly it serves
as a poem for dark and dangerous times, acknowledging that
many felt lost and abandoned after the Reformation cut them
off from the Church, either because they were Protestants
and so had to work out their own path to salvation, or because
they were Catholics and no longer had a Church to guide
them unless they adopted a perilous and dangerous course
of action.

Donne had lamented the lack of a Church to guide him
from relatively early in his life. Satire 3, 'Kind pity chokes
my spleen', written in the mid-1590s, laments the confusing
state of religion in his lifetime. The speaker wonders where
he might be able to find the truth:

> 'Seek true religion.' O where? Myrius,
> Thinking her unhoused here, and fled from us,
> Seeks her at Rome – there, because he doth know
> That she was there a thousand years ago;
> He loves the rags so as we here obey
> The state-cloth where the prince sate yesterday.
> Crantz to such brave loves will not be enthralled,
> But loves her only, who at Gèneva is called
> Religion: plain, simple, sullen, young,
> Contemptuous; yet unhandsome, as among
> Lecherous humours there is one that judges
> No wenches wholesome but coarse country drudges.

Graius stays still at home here, and because
Some preachers – vile, ambitious bawds – and laws ·
Still new, like fashions – bid him think that she
Which dwells with us is only perfect, he
Embraceth her whom his godfathers will
Tender to him, being tender, as wards still
Take such wives as their guardians offer, or
Pay values. Careless Phrygius doth abhor
All, because all cannot be good, as one,
Knowing some women whores, dares marry none.
Graccus loves all as one, and thinks that so,
As women do in divers countries go
In divers habits, yet are still one kind,
So doth, so is Religion; and this blind-
ness too much light breeds; but unmoved, thou
Of force must one, and forced, but one allow;
And the right; ask thy father which is she,
Let him ask his: though Truth and Falsehood be
Near twins, yet Truth a little elder is.
Be busy to seek her; believe me this:
He's not of none, nor worst, that seeks the best.
T'adore, or scorn an image, or protest,
May all be bad; doubt wisely. In strange way
To stand enquiring right, is not to stray,
To sleep, or run wrong, is. On a huge hill,
Craggèd and steep, Truth stands, and he that will
Reach her, about must, and about must go,
And what the hill's suddenness resists, win so.
(43–82)

Donne's speaker surveys the different approaches to religion, before concluding that none provide a direct route to the truth, his analysis gradually shifting towards the comparison between choosing a form of faith and a wife.

Myrius (perhaps suggesting 'myrrh' and a devotion to ancient rituals) wants a return to Rome, but the desire to re-establish a religion that was properly practised a millennium ago indicates the impossibility of doing so, and may also gesture towards a Protestant understanding that the primitive Church functioned properly until it was corrupted by Roman rituals and practices.[34] Myrius attaches great spiritual value to ephemera, such as rags (presumably scraps of saints' clothing or cloth that absorbed – or was said to have absorbed – the blood of martyrs), but these are no more significant than the 'state-cloth' (throne) where the monarch recently sat, treated with reverence by her awed subjects. This carefully balanced line criticizes both Catholic superstition and those who imagine that a Protestant monarch is also divinely sanctioned, the speaker's scepticism establishing the tone of what is to follow. Crantz (the name may imply a pious Dutch schismatic) wants to take a different path and instead admires Geneva, the theocracy where Calvin holds sway. In sharp contrast to Catholicism and the Church of England, this form of religion is austere and unattractive. Moreover, whereas Catholicism is old and established, Calvinism is new, which, given its character, does not bode well for the future of Christianity if it develops, grows and attracts large numbers of converts.

As the sexual comparison indicates, Calvinism would appear to generate repression of desire and perversity, its adherents claiming to prefer what they find ugly to what they know is beautiful, which cannot be what God has planned for mankind. Graius ('Greek', implying weakness and the desire to adopt the path of least resistance) stays put, makes little effort and follows whichever way the wind blows. He is persuaded by the (weak) arguments of unscrupulous and ambitious local divines that either the queen or the established Church ('she') are the best they can be and no possible change is needed, a complacency that is surely not what God had intended. Phrygius ('the Trojan', either ironically referring to Paris' abduction of Helen or to the Phrygian cult of the goddess Cybele, whose members castrated themselves and so felt no desire)[35] is the direct opposite of Graius. He despises everything and simply cannot believe that there is a way to discover and understand true religion. Graccus ('priest of Mars', referred to in Juvenal's second satire, the principal model for Donne's scathing and angry satires)[36] is someone who cannot distinguish between anything and so has no understanding of the meaning of religion, adopting a dogmatic pluralism that assumes that religious belief is culturally specific. The problem that Graccus creates is an excess of light, imagining that more of the world is working according to God's plan than it is, the opposite view of that of the speaker in Holy Sonnet 4, who cannot imagine that God will grant mankind grace. As the narrator pointedly informs the reader, an excess of light produces blindness.

Having surveyed the different (false) approaches to the problem of religion, Donne's speaker reminds us that although truth is hard to distinguish from falsehood, it must always come first. Truth and falsehood may be twins – the metaphor moving the discussion from desire and the choice of marriage partner to its purpose, the production of children – but truth has to be the elder. Therefore, the views of Phrygius and Graccus, the one believing that everything is good, the other everything to be bad, cannot be right. Truth may be hard to uncover but that is no excuse for giving up, because anyone at all acquainted with the Bible knows that the path to righteousness is a narrow one that is hard to follow. Truth stands on a high, inaccessible peak, a vivid demonstration of how exhausting and relentless the search for religious revelation must be.

The passage demonstrates that Donne's views of religion were largely consistent throughout his life, which suggests that the notion of a sudden change of faith after the death of his brother may well be mistaken.[37] The satire shows how keen and wide-ranging Donne's perception of religious dispute was from a relatively early age and how clear was his theological thinking. He was undoubtedly carefully surveying and absorbing the writings of the Church fathers as well as the disputes between Catholics and Protestants from his late teens onwards.[38] Donne argues that religion is incredibly difficult to understand properly and, although there is surely a right way to envisage God's plans for mankind, it is not easy to find it, or to represent it correctly even if one does. He is sceptical of the claims of the Church of England, the Catholic Church and the Reformed Church in Geneva, as well as those who claim that all religious positions are equally valid and that all are similarly mistaken. Satire 3 argues that even though Christians are left alone in the world without a Church to guide them to the truth, they cannot give up their quest.

The corollary of the argument of Satire 3 is found in *Pseudo-Martyr*, a sustained argument that loyalty to the state should enable Christians to practise their own religion in private. It does not follow that anything goes; rather, Donne's point is that coercion does not help in religious matters and individuals should be left alone to explore faith – with proper guidance, should they seek it – as best they can. His position could be seen as Protestant, accepting the right of the monarch to rule, and he has been labelled an absolutist.[39] However, it is an error to assume that the radical separation of Church and state is a particularly Protestant understanding of religious and political organization derived from Luther, as is often assumed.[40] We should instead regard such ideas as a post-Reformation way of thinking that was adopted by Catholics as well as Protestants. Edmund Campion, the Jesuit martyr, argued at his trial that his mission to England had not threatened the queen, as he and his fellow Jesuits sought only to influence the spiritual and not the political views of people.[41] Donne consistently made the case, in many different ways, that the hard work of understanding religion needed to be undertaken by individuals free to debate matters openly and so find the path to truth.

In Donne's lifetime such aims could be no more than pious hopes, as he lived through the repressive regime designed to combat the Jesuit missions of the 1580s; the fear of civil war and the succession crisis of the 1590s; the Gunpowder Plot and the resulting Oath of Allegiance; more than a decade of the Thirty Years War in Europe; the accession of Charles I in 1625 and the drift towards absolutism after the king dissolved Parliament in 1629. We know a relatively large amount about Donne's life and he wrote a great deal on religious subjects, but we are mostly in the dark about his religious views beyond his desire for religious toleration.[42] There is no general agreement regarding what he thought about the sacraments; church furniture or priests' vestments; free will and predestination; ceremony; ritual and order of service; the liturgy; the translation of the Bible; and so on. We know little about what he thought apart from his stated beliefs in the need to preserve Church unity; for the Church to have strong secular leadership; and for individuals to be left free to explore the mysteries of the faith themselves, the basic conditions for Christian thinking and not the theological substance itself.

The sermons demonstrate the carefully balanced nature of Donne's theological style: on the one hand explaining the nature of Christian belief, and on the other avoiding a commitment to a doctrinal position because faith is by definition beyond reason. A good example is the sermon preached on Easter Day 1628 at St Paul's Cathedral, on the well-known biblical text 1 Corinthians 13:12: 'For now we see through a glasse darkly; but then face to face: now I know in part; but then shall I know even as also I am knowne' (King James translation). The sermon opens with a meditation on the time signified by the biblical verse: now and then. What we can comprehend now has to be understood in terms of what we will understand in the future (then), when we can actually witness the face of God:

the *Then*, the time of *seeing face to face*, and *knowing as we are knowne*, is intended of that time, which we celebrate

> this day, the day of Resurrection, the day of Judgement,
> the day of the actuall possession of the next life.[43]

On that day we will have 'perfect sight of all', because now we can only see through a darkened glass. Donne has returned to his familiar refrain, that we will know and understand very little until we die and are reunited with God, our life on earth being a transitory, testing phase which prepares us for the afterlife. He also refers to the Day of Judgement, indicating that the 'then' is not far from the 'now', and that will be the time when the union of the body and soul is properly achieved. Until then our knowledge will be limited and there is only so much that we can hope to understand, so it is far better to wait for proper revelation:

> And here we know God *In aenigmate* [as a riddle, an
> allegory], says our Text, *Darkly*, (so we translate it) that
> is, by obscure representations, and therefore it is called
> a *knowledge but in part*; But in Heaven, our sight is *face
> to face*, And our knowledge is *to know, as we are knowne*.

On earth we have to rely on our reason and senses, which are limited, but in heaven 'our medium is the Patefaction [open declaration], the Manifestation, the Revelation of god himselfe, and our light is the light of glory. And then for our knowledge of God there, God himself is all.' The light of God replaces the darkness that obscures things on earth.

What we see on earth is 'a representation onely', but it is enough for us to know 'that a God there is'. The glass that enables us to see God is better than a reflection in water as

we see via the light of 'Naturall Reason' and we must use our
faculties to see God in the world, which is 'the Theatre that
represents God, and every where man may, nay must see him'.[44]
Donne accepts but sees the limitations of the long-standing
idea that we can see God revealed in the Book of Nature.[45] He
selects an eccentric list of animals normally marginalized in
bestiaries to demonstrate the truth of the analogy and its
limitations:

> If every gnat that flies were an Arch-angell, all that
> could but tell me, that there is a God: and the poorest
> worme that creeps, tells me that. If I should aske the
> Basilisk [mythical beast, part serpent, part rooster,
> capable of killing with its stare] how camest thou by
> those killing eyes, he would tell me, Thy God made
> me so; And if I should aske the Slow-worme, how
> camest thou to be without eyes, he would tell me, Thy
> God made me so. The Cedar is no better a glasse to
> see God in, than the Hyssope upon the wall; all things
> that are, are equally removed from being nothing; and
> whatsoever hath any beeing, is by that very being, a
> glasse in which we see God, who is the roote, and the
> fountaine of all being. (p. 224)

The world tells us everything and nothing: it proves the
existence of God because he is the author of every creature,
however odd or unusual. However, it does not enable us to
understand anything in particular about the nature of the
Creator, which, Donne implies, is the common mistake that
so many over-eager theologians make. Only when we die

and our souls are reunited with God can we understand such things. The world is not designed to provide mankind with certainty, and it is only atheists who want such false security. The world will tell us that there is a God and that it does not make sense without an understanding that he exists, but it can tell us nothing about his nature, which is why there are so many possible explanations that we can reach using our speculative reason and powers of deduction, but we will only know the truth when we die. The glass is too dark for us to see properly before then: what we have is the Church and scripture to guide us and inspire us to accept the true faith. Only by truly loving ourselves can we love God properly, a union of creator and creation, and only by recognizing that our powers of reason are too weak to understand the world fully will we be able to understand what it can tell us about God.

In a sermon preached two years earlier, Donne had expanded on his vision of what happens to the soul after death. This was one of the sermons delivered in his role as royal chaplain on 18 April 1626 about John 14:2: 'In my Father's house are many mansions; if it were not so, I would have told you' (King James Version).[46] Donne explains that after death all the souls will be united in harmony by God:

> We shall have an association with the Angels, and such a one, as we shall be such as they. We shall have an association with the Saints, and not onely so, to be such as they, but to be they; And with all *who come from the East, and from the West, and from the North, and from the South, and sit down with Abraham, and Isaac, and Jacob in the kingdome of heaven.* Where we shall be so far from being enemies

to one another, as that we shall not be strangers to one
another: And so far from envying one another, as that
all that every one hath, shall be every others possession:
where all soules shall be so intirely knit together, as if
all were but one soule, and God so intirely knit to every
soule, as if there were as many Gods as soules. (p. 54)

This is – yet another – rhetorical tour de force, as Donne
imagines the progress of the soul to heaven, where it will join
all the other souls in heaven, the finest of God's mansions.
There is the familiar image of the globe, with souls hasten-
ing from all corners to join the patriarchs in heaven. No
longer will there be conflict as there is on earth but the souls
will unite, joining with angels and saints – such distinctions,
Donne indicates, only make sense when seen from the earth,
as a means to inspire mankind to worship God. Donne's
apocalyptic imagery imagines the end of everything in heaven
as God binds all together.

Donne is almost exclusively concerned with his soul in
his writings, because it is his and one can only really know
one's own soul. However, in *The Anniversaries*, two long poems
written just after *Pseudo-Martyr*, Donne meditates about the
state of the soul as the world decays and hastens towards its
last days. The poems mourn the death of Elizabeth Drury
(1596–1610), daughter of Donne's patron and friend Sir
Robert Drury (1575–1615), a soldier and politician with whom
Donne travelled in Europe in the years 1611–12.[47] Donne uses
the sad event to reflect on the nature of the world in 'The
First Anniversary: An Anatomy of the World' and the inspiration provided by Elizabeth in 'The Second Anniversary: Of

the Progress of the Soul', the two poems published together with connecting poems by Donne's friend Joseph Hall (1574–1656) in 1612, two years after Elizabeth's death.

The opening lines of the first poem urge readers to use Elizabeth's example to think about themselves and the state of their own soul:

> When that rich soul which to her heaven is gone
> Whom all they celebrate who know they've one
> (For who is sure he hath a soul, unless
> It see and judge and follow worthiness,
> And by deeds praise it? He who doth not this,
> May lodge an inmate soul, but 'tis not his) (1–6).

Donne argues that only through self-reflection can one understand that one has a soul. It might be possible to recognize that another creature has one, but only through

Nicholas Stone, funeral monument of Elizabeth Drury, All Saints Church, Hawstead, Suffolk.

an empathy and a realization that one wishes to copy the behaviour and actions of a virtuous soul can one know that one has a soul oneself – lines that explain why Donne places so much emphasis on himself and his own experience. Elizabeth's soul is largely unknowable as only her own realization that she has a soul as other people do can make sense of her existence and only God can really know the state of the individual soul. In order to reflect on Elizabeth's virtue and godliness, Donne has to understand her effect on others and, of course, on him in particular, judging as far as he is able that her virtue stands out in a wicked world and has surely ensured her a place in heaven. Elizabeth's death has been a merciful release but her ethereal presence serves to inspire the godly:

> Though she which did inanimate and fill
> The world be gone, yet in this last long night
> Her ghost doth walk, that is, a glimmering light,
> A faint weak love of virtue and of good,
> Reflects from her on them which understood
> Her worth (68–73)

Souls are inspired by other souls just as Christians are inspired by saints, as Donne acknowledges in 'The Second Anniversary' (512–13).

Elizabeth stands as a reminder that the only true sustenance is 'The supernatural food, religion' (line 188), and that nature is in a state of permanent decay and cannot be trusted. The most celebrated lines in the poem are often cited to suggest that Donne is at odds with the exciting new developments

in science that were taking place in his lifetime,[48] and which
he was keen to follow elsewhere in his writing:

> And new philosophy calls all in doubt:
> The element of fire is quite put out,
> The Sun is lost, and th'Earth, and no man's wit
> Can well direct him where to look for it;
> And freely men confess that this world's spent,
> When in the planets and the firmament
> They seek so many new; they see that this
> Is crumbled out again t'his atomies.
> 'Tis all in pieces, all coherence gone,
> All just supply, and all relation (205–14)

The emphasis of the lines is not that such new knowledge
necessarily creates confusion and inspires doubt, but that
it is not yet understood and has increased a sense that one
cannot look to the natural world for any certainties. In such
times, Donne argues, we should turn to the certainties of religion inspired by virtuous Christians such as Elizabeth, whose
example can supply more certainty and guidance (even as
Donne acknowledges that we cannot know the state of other
souls). Lines soon after these reflections on the challenge of
empirical science surely reinforce this reading:

> She that was best and first original
> Of all fair copies, and the general
> Steward to Fate; she whose rich eyes and breast
> Gilt the West Indies, and perfumed the East,
> Whose having breathed in this world, did bestow

> Spice on those isles, and bade them still smell so,
> And that rich Indie which doth gold inter,
> Is but as single money, coined from her;
> She to whom this world must itself refer,
> As suburbs or the microcosm of her;
> She, she is dead; she's dead: when thou know'st this,
> Thou know'st how lame a cripple this world is.
>   (227–37)

The great riches of the earth, brought back from remote, exotic lands, are also worthless now that Elizabeth is dead because everything imitates her. Coins stand for things of value as the medium of exchange, but Elizabeth is the original copy, fixed in permanent value as the perfect imitation that remains stable but diminishes as it is copied, which is why Donne describes her, in characteristically paradoxical fashion, as 'single money', something that can be imitated, but at the expense of losing its precious and unique value. Without her in it, the world decays and loses its lustre so that every birth is really a death: 'Springtimes were common cradles, but are tombs; / And false conceptions fill the general wombs' (384–5). Of course, Donne knows this is true and the poem concludes 'Heaven keeps souls, / The grave keeps bodies' (473–4), but Elizabeth's death throws it into stark relief and reminds him that the proper object of study is devotion to God in order to save one's soul.

Having established the false, ephemeral and rotten nature of the world, 'The Second Anniversary' charts the journey of the virtuous soul up to heaven. In addressing his own soul Donne is aiming to speak for every man and woman. He

urges the soul to be 'insatiate' (45) in its search for God's love
and to 'Forget this rotten world' (49) and concentrate on
heaven. Elizabeth's death reminds us that 'though a good man
hath / Title to Heav'n' (149–50) it is 'Death must usher, and
unlock the door' (156), a message repeated later in his sermons on death. The soul is infected by the body, 'Bedded and
bathed in all his ordures, dwells / So foully as our souls i'their
first-built cells' (171–2), which is why Elizabeth, who fortu-
nately escaped from hers so early, stands as a beacon to guide
us, never having been truly corrupted by sin. Donne hopes
that he can follow her example and that his soul 'Return not
. . . from this ecstasy / And meditation of what thou shalt be'
(321–2). The poem concludes by imagining the journey of
Elizabeth's soul up through heaven to the ranks of the most
virtuous of God's servants:

> Up to those Patriarchs, which did longer sit
> Expecting Christ than they've enjoyed him yet;
> Up to those Prophets, which now gladly see

Francesco Botticini, *The Assumption of the Virgin, c.* 1475–6, tempera on wood.

Their prophesies grown to be history;
Up to th' Apostles, who did bravely run
All the Sun's course with more light than the Sun;
Up to those Martyrs, who did calmly bleed,
Oil to th'Apostles' lamps, dew to their seed;
Up to those Virgins, who thought that almost
They made joint-tenants with the Holy Ghost,
If they to any should His temple give;
Up, up, for in that squadron there doth live
She who hath carried thither new degrees
(As to their number) to their dignities (345–58).

This vision of a hierarchical heaven has its roots in traditional images of heaven carefully populated with distinct
levels of angels (as in Francesco Botticini's *The Assumption of
the Virgin*). Furthermore, it would appear to be at odds with
Donne's vision of heaven as a union of all souls in his sermon
on John 14:2, a reminder that representations for particular
purposes and in specific contexts cannot necessarily be read
as doctrinal statements. Here, Elizabeth stands as the example of a good and virtuous soul, reminding Donne's readers
that the purpose of life can only be understood through
death: the example of that life after its death for others, and
the realization of the fate of the soul for the individual when
they die. Donne is undoubtedly an egocentric writer, but that
strong sense of self also charts the progress of the soul.

William Larkin, *Lucy Harington, Countess of Bedford, Married to Edward Russel, Earl of Bedford*, 1610s, oil on canvas.

THREE

Sexuality

onne is probably most famous as a poet of bold and explicit sexuality, his daring 'metaphysical' style transforming the conventions of English lyric poetry.[1] His reputation is not without reason: after all, the author of 'The Flea' and 'To His Mistress Going to Bed' is clearly an erotic poet, and he certainly had a reputation as a ladies' man when young.[2] However, considerable caution is required when thinking about Donne and sex.

Most Renaissance English poets produced bawdy verse at some point, usually when they were young. Shakespeare's *Venus and Adonis* (1593) appears to have been consumed by a large number of young male readers and established his reputation as an erotic, Ovidian poet, colouring his literary identity into the seventeenth century.[3] Christopher Marlowe wrote a number of erotic poems, notably his translations of Ovid's elegies, as well as the more obviously pornographic *Hero and Leander* (1598).[4] Thomas Nashe wrote the notorious and widely circulated manuscript poem 'The Choice of Valentines', also known as 'Nashe's Dildo'.[5] The poetry of Edmund Spenser (1552/4–1599), the dominant literary poet of the 1590s, is often highly erotic.[6] Furthermore, there are a large number of less well-known poets, such as Barnabe Barnes, known for their ribald, sometimes rather tasteless, verse.[7]

In the 1590s there was a fashion for highly sexualized Ovidian poetry and Donne, like most of his contemporaries, whether through inclination, the demands of patrons or the desire to follow literary fashions and learn how to write, produced a number of examples. We have to be careful in assuming that what Donne wrote was what he thought.[8] Many of his poems, as I have argued in the previous chapter, some of them frank and erotic, were probably written for his wife and may have been designed only for circulation among a select group of readers. Therefore, we often have no real idea how Donne's poetry about women, unless it appears to have been written about Ann, can be read in terms of his own experience.

The misogynistic lyric 'Twickenham Garden' is a good example. The poem's agenda would seem to be clear enough and similar to other poems that appeared in *Songs and Sonnets* such as 'Go and catch a falling star' and 'Air and Angels'. The title derives from the first edition of Donne's poems (1639), so it could well be authorial.[9] Twickenham Park was leased to Lucy Russell, née Harington, Countess of Bedford, in 1607. Donne was one of the many authors she supported (others were Ben Jonson, George Chapman, Michael Drayton and Samuel Daniel), so the poem can probably be dated to 1608–10.[10] It was therefore written not long after many of Donne's 'marriage poems' and, more significantly, for a woman patron, who presumably read the work that advertised itself as having been written in her house.[11] This spring poem is spoken by a neglected lover who sees his fortune at odds with the traditional rites of spring and so roundly curses all woman-kind in the final stanza:

> Hither, with crystal vials, lovers, come
>> And take my tears, which are love's wine,
>> And try your mistress' tears at home;
> For all are false that taste not just like mine.
>> Alas, hearts do not in eyes shine,
> Nor can you more judge woman's thoughts by tears,
>> Than by her shadow, what she wears.
> O perverse sex, where none is true but she,
> Who's therefore true, because her truth kills me.
> (19–27)

Even if this poem did not appear to be addressed to – or, at the very least, connected with – the Countess of Bedford, it is hard not to read it as a witty joke, exposing ridiculous male attitudes to women. The paradox that women are so false that the truest woman is a false one is part of the standard misogyny that blamed women's inconstancy on Eve's inability to resist the serpent, a prejudice that all educated men would have known (and not necessarily shared).[12] The intemperate diatribe of the bruised male ego who is at odds with the rites of spring was revisited later by Donne in 'A Nocturnal upon St Lucy's Day', a further sign that 'Twickenham Garden' should not be taken at face value.[13] Rather, the poem would appear to be satirical, a dramatic monologue that was, one suspects, designed to be read by men and women, who would have enjoyed the exaggerated role-playing that it involves.[14]

Donne was always aware that he was writing within a poetic tradition and for a sophisticated audience who understood his references and could be persuaded by his complicated and controversial arguments.[15] He was acutely conscious of the different types of audience he addressed: sermons and works such as *Pseudo-Martyr* were for larger, mixed audiences; his poetry and works such as *Biathanatos* were for more restricted, intimate groups of readers. 'Twickenham Garden', according to this logic, may well have meant one thing to early readers using a manuscript and quite another to many readers of the printed edition of the poems. The same might be said of 'To His Mistress Going to Bed', a much earlier poem (probably 1593–6) that is replete with Ovidian sexual energy and tension, as the lover demands that his mistress undress for him and describes the process, real or imagined, for the reader. Ovid is keenly interested in women's bodies in his poetry, and he recounts an undressing in the fifth elegy:

> I grabbed the dress; it didn't hide much,
> but she fought to keep it,
>
> only half-heartedly though.
> Victory was easy, a self-betrayal.
>
> There she stood, faultless beauty
> in front of me, naked.
>
> Shoulders and arms challenging eyes and fingers.
> Nipples firmly demanding attention.

Breasts in high relief above the smooth belly.
Long and slender waist. Thighs of a girl.

Why list perfection?
I hugged her tight.

The rest can be imagined – we fell asleep.
Such afternoons are rare.[16]

Corinna's rapid denuding bears little comparison to Donne's lengthy, lecherous description of his mistress undressing, as the poet extends the familiar form of the blazon (the poet's description of his mistress's body) as far as he can. Donne is filling in the gaps left by Ovid's narrator's question, 'Why list perfection?' Whereas Corinna's clothes are off after a token struggle, in 'To His Mistress Going to Bed', Donne's lover luxuriates in the act of the woman stripping, making use of the tried and tested comparison between the arts of love and the arts of war, implicit in Ovid's erotic writings:

The foe oft-times, having the foe in sight,
Is tired with standing though they never fight.
Off with that girdle, like Heaven's zone glist'ring,
But a far fairer world encompassing?
Unpin that spangled breastplate, which you wear,
That th'eyes of busy fools may be stopped there!
Unlace yourself, for that harmonious chime
Tells me from you, that now 'tis your bed time.
Off with that happy busk, whom I envy
That still can be and still can stand so nigh! (3–12)

Donne is deliberately overgoing Ovid in the force, extent and daring of his erotic poetry, perhaps responding to requests, such as that made in Sir Philip Sidney's *An Apologie for Poetrie* (*c.* 1580, published 1595), that English writers try to rival the cultural achievements of the ancients.[17] Donne's poem, which was censored in the early editions of his poetry and not printed until after the Restoration, makes Ovid seem rather tame in comparison.[18]

Donne's poem can be compared to other works written at about the same time, many of which seek to use Ovidian subjects to titillate, challenge and amuse the reader, deliberately pushing the boundaries of what could be represented in literary works.[19] Shakespeare's *Venus and Adonis* narrated the stock pornographic theme of the sexually voracious older woman seducing a younger man, but makes the subject as much ludicrous as erotic. The goddess of love makes clear the opportunities that are available to the handsome youth:

> 'Fondling,' she saith, 'since I have hemm'd thee here
> Within the circuit of this ivory pale,
> I'll be a park, and thou shalt be my deer;
> Feed where thou wilt, on mountain or in dale;
>   Graze on my lips, and if those hills be dry,
>   Stray lower, where the pleasant fountains lie.

> 'Within this limit is relief enough,
> Sweet bottom-grass and high delightful plain,
> Round rising hillocks, brakes obscure and rough,
> To shelter thee from tempest and from rain:

Then be my deer, since I am such a park,
   No dog shall rouse thee, though a thousand
     bark.'[20]

However, Adonis is far more interested in hunting the fierce, tusked boar (which provides the poem with obvious homosexual hints), and the humiliated goddess is reduced to the most basic of seduction tactics, which, unfortunately, do little to slake her unsatisfied desire:

And on his neck her yoking arms she throws.
   She sinketh down, still hanging by his neck;
   He on her belly falls, she on her back.

Now is she in the very lists of love,
Her champion mounted for the hot encounter.
All is imaginary she doth prove;
He will not manage her, although he mount her:
   That worse than Tantalus' is her annoy,
   To clip Elysium and to lack her joy. (592–600)

The poem would appear to balance pornographic fantasy and representation with earthy humour, perhaps the main reason why it could be published and sold well as a printed book.[21] The same might also be said of Thomas Nashe's even more daring 'The Choice of Valentines', which was not published but did circulate widely in manuscript when it was written, around 1592.[22] Nashe describes the encounter between a lecherous youth and a prostitute using similar language to Shakespeare:

Oh heaven, and paradize are all but toyes,
Compar'd with this sight, I now behould,
   Which well might keepe a man from being olde.
A prettie rysing wombe without a weame [belly],
   That shone as bright as anie silver streame;
And bare out lyke the bending of an hill,
   At whose decline a fountaine dwelleth still,
That hath his mouth besett with uglie bryers
   Resembling much a duskie nett of wyres.
A loftie buttock barred with azure veine's
   Whose comelie swelling, when my hand distreine's,
Or wanton checketh with a harmeless stype,
   It makes the fruites of love eftsoone be rype;
And pleasure pluckt too tymelie from the stemme
   To dye ere it hath seene Jerusalem.[23]

Shakespeare and Nashe adopt a similarly knowing tone
and style of bucolic imagery to represent the female body, one

Giorgione and Titian, *Sleeping Venus, c.* 1508–10, oil on canvas.

replete with euphemisms that are easily decoded and so draw
attention to the erotic nature of their subject. As in *Venus and
Adonis*, the sexual encounter is represented in a humorous
manner so that the poem can be read as a light-hearted parody
of intimate behaviour as well as for its obviously voyeuristic
qualities. And, as with Shakespeare's poem, Nashe undoubtedly takes his cue from Ovid, whose speaker fails to rise to the
occasion in one of the later elegies.[24] The eager youth proves
rather over-eager and no amount of amorous activity will save
the day:

> With Oh, and Oh, she itching moues hir hipps,
>   And to and fro, full lightlie starts and skips.
> She jerks hir leggs, and sprauleth with hir heeles,
>   No tongue maie tell the solace that she feeles.
> I faint, I yeald; Oh death rock me a-sleepe.
> (199–203)

His partner is forced to turn to a prosthetic device to avoid
the frustration that Venus experiences.

Such poems enable us to contextualize Donne's 'Mistress
Going to Bed' elegy, which reads like a work that pushes the
boundaries of literary taste as far as it can. While Ovid concentrates on mood and actions rather than description, and
Shakespeare and Nashe employ a series of ingenious metaphors to represent sexualized nudity, Donne's speaker uses
similar imagery to revel in his vision of the female body and
draws attention to what he can see, sharing as much as possible
with the reader as the woman undresses:

Your gown's going off, such beauteous state reveals
As when from flow'ry meads th'hill's shadow steals.
Off with your wiry coronet, and shew
The hairy diadem which on you doth grow!
Now off with those shoes and then safely tread
In this – Love's hallowed temple – this soft bed!
In such white robes Heaven's angels used to be
Received by men: thou, angel bring'st with thee
A heaven like Mahomet's Paradise; and though
Ill spirits walk in white, we eas'ly know
By this these angels from an evil sprite:
Those set our hairs, but these our flesh upright.
(13–24)

The female body is imagined in terms of the natural world:
perhaps Donne is thinking of an image of a naked Venus in
a pastoral landscape? Shakespeare and Nashe produced similar images in their poems and Donne's writing builds carefully
on an Ovidian tradition to draw attention to what the speaker
can see (see the *Sleeping Venus* attributed to Giorgione). The
'hairy diadem' refers most obviously to her head, but, when
coupled with the description of hills and flowery meadows
after she has removed her gown, makes the reader aware of
other hair on her body. The reference to 'Mahomet's Paradise'
is also explicitly sexual, as Islam was closely associated with
sexual licence and Christians believed not only that Mahomet
and his father were promiscuous, but that their heaven was
imagined as a place of unparalleled sexual pleasure.[25] The sly
pseudo-theological joke completes the section and continues
the theme of hair: evil spirits are hair-raising but the angel

in her white underwear causes motion in another part of
the body.

The next lines, the most celebrated in the poem, provide
a political subtext:

> Licence my roving hands, and let them go
> Behind, before, above, between, below!
> O my America! my new-found land!
> My kingdom, safeliest when with one man manned!
> My mine of precious stones! My empery!
> How blessed am I in this discovering thee! (25–30)

The lover casts himself as the imperial ruler so the lady
becomes his conquered territory. The lines signal Donne's
interest in the exploration of the New World, in particular
the exploits of Sir Walter Raleigh. Raleigh sailed with Donne
on the voyage to Cadiz (June–August 1596) and, again, on
the Azores-bound voyages (July–October 1597), which might
indicate that the elegy was written just before or soon after
the expeditions.[26] If so, then they may not be without some
wit, drawing attention to Donne's westward enterprise, one
that did not actually reach America.

Furthermore, Donne's speaker casts himself as a potent
man ravishing the female New World, a stock image of colonial propaganda.[27] However, English colonial exploits in the
1590s were not quite as they were represented in Donne's
poem. They were undertaken under the auspices of a queen
and the most significant colony established in the Americas
was named Virginia in her honour, as a sign that the colonial
adventurers she sent out were able to control themselves and

plant the land as she would have wished, in a measured and regulated fashion.[28] If the poem was written after 1596 then there may well be an allusion to Raleigh's famous description of Guiana as

Unknown artist, *Sir Walter Ralegh* (*Raleigh*), 1588, oil on panel.

a Countrey that hath yet her Maydenhead, never sackt, turned, nor wrought; the face of the earth hath not been torne, nor the vertue and salt of the soyle spent by manurance, the graves have not been opened for gold, the mines not broken with sledges, nor their Images puld down out of their temples. It hath never been enterd by any armie of strength, and never conquered or possessed by any Christian Prince.[29]

Raleigh's text deliberately advertises the proper restraint of the English colonists, signalling his own temperance and ability to control his appetites. Raleigh was seeking to rehabilitate himself after his secret marriage to Elizabeth Throckmorton, one of Elizabeth's ladies-in-waiting, which had infuriated the queen, who banished them to their estates

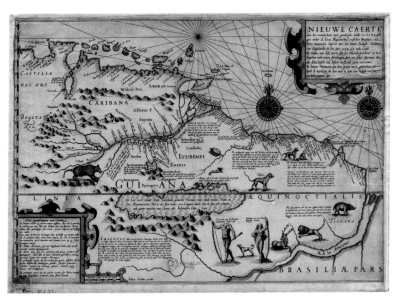

Jodocus Hondius, after Walter Raleigh, *New Map of the Wonderful, Large and Rich Land of Guiana*, 1598, hand-coloured map.

in Sherborne.[30] He was also deliberately representing English colonial ventures in direct contrast to those of the Spanish, who were notorious throughout Europe for their greed for gold and lack of respect for indigenous peoples, and for leaving a trail of destruction in the wake of their colonial ventures.[31]

We ought not to assume, therefore, that Donne's eager young lover is to be taken any more seriously than Nashe's hapless protagonist, or that the poem lacks the irony and humour of *Venus and Adonis*. Like Shakespeare's poem, which shows how dangerously empty a life based on the pleasures of the flesh must be in the face of death, Donne's elegy contains more serious themes too. The final section compares men and women to books, concluding with the bawdy image of the naked man 'cover'ng' (a word with obvious sexual significance in this period) the naked woman, teaching her as well as making the physical form of the book complete.[32] In employing the image Donne returns to his familiar obsession with the soul:

> Full nakedness, all joys are due to thee:
> As souls unbodied, bodies unclothed must be
> To taste whole joys. Gems which you women use
> Are as At'lanta's balls cast in men's views,
> That when a fool's eye lighteth on a gem,
> His earthly soul may covet theirs not them. (33–8)

At one obvious level this is a quibble, to be read alongside the witty but insubstantial and unpersuasive arguments made throughout 'The Flea'. The first three lines quoted here claim that souls do not need to be unclothed like bodies or be in the presence of naked figures in order to combine. Elsewhere Donne uses diametrically opposed images to make similar points about the need for the union of souls. In 'A Valediction Forbidding Mourning', probably written around 1605 and so another one of the group of 'marriage poems', the speaker claims that it is their separation that proves the lovers' proper union, as their intimate connection stretches to produce something astonishingly beautiful and incomprehensible:

> Dull sublunary lovers' love
> >   (Whose soul is sense) cannot admit
> Absence, because it doth remove
> >   Those things which elemented it.
>
> But we by a love so much refined
> >   That ourselves know not what it is,
> Inter-assured of the mind,
> >   Care less, eyes, lips, and hands to miss.
>
> Our two souls therefore, which are one,
> >   Though I must go, endure not yet
> A breach, but an expansion,
> >   Like gold to airy thinness beat. (13–24)

In this poem the lovers' souls are united without the need for physical contact because they have a bond that cannot be broken, elevating them above other lovers.

Donne is employing Neoplatonic imagery in both the Valediction and the elegy, but to make quite different points:

in the elegy the lovers require physical union in order to consummate their love; in 'A Valediction' it is their absence that cements their bond. In the elegy, physical love leads to spiritual love, while in 'A Valediction' the existence of spiritual love demonstrates that physical love is not required. Donne's poetry is often analysed in terms of Neoplatonic thought: the belief, inspired by thinkers such as Giovanni Pico della Mirandola and Marsilio Ficino, as well as Petrarch, that earthly values and earthly love are simply shadows of a higher reality, pointing towards the need to think about more spiritual, often Christian, values.[33] What his poetry actually reveals is that he was prepared to use such ideas in a pragmatic and open-minded manner. Neoplatonism, for Donne, is less a philosophy than a metaphysical idea, one that a rhetorically sophisticated speaker can employ to make a particular point.[34] Donne was far too sophisticated a theologian to parrot such simplistic notions and we do him a major disservice in reducing his poetry to a straightforward doctrine that can be easily decoded.

However, what the elegy does make clear is that a straightforwardly Ovidian sex poem cannot be taken at face value, and that same complexity is also present in the works of other thoughtful poets who write about physical love, such as Nashe and Shakespeare. In comparing himself and his lover to books and souls Donne shows that even at such times of carnal appetite human actions have a divine mystery that needs to be considered and analysed. Sex, after all, could never simply be a recreational activity for Donne. It was designed by God to produce children – the Donnes had twelve – and the emission of male semen was thought to diminish the limited life forces within the body, which is why the male orgasm is considered a 'little death'.[35] In Donne's era women were thought to conceive only if they experienced sexual pleasure.[36] Sex was always a serious business, whether as something to be celebrated, condemned or controlled.[37]

Some effort is required to read Donne's lines, which make the point that sex cannot be taken as lightly as the speaker in 'To His Mistress Going to Bed' imagines. While the first lines argue that sex offers a direct passage to the union of souls, the second sentence is more ambiguous. Are the gems that women use those that the lady wears? Or might they stand for the beauty of her body? The myth of 'At'lanta's balls' is the story of the beautiful virgin huntress's unwillingness to marry any of her suitors, undoubtedly taken from Ovid's *Metamorphoses*, where the story is told at length.[38] She was able to run quickly, and so stated that she would only marry someone who could defeat her in a race, the losers being put to death. The besotted Hippomenes consulted Aphrodite, who gave him three apples, and he used these to distract Atlanta, eventually defeating her when she stooped to pick up the third one. Their story did not end happily, however, and because Hippomenes failed to thank Aphrodite properly for her help, the couple were turned into lions when they stopped to make love in Cybele's temple.

The comparison of the gems to the apples that Aphrodite gives Hippomenes reminds readers that sex is never just sex. Who has put them there and what purpose do they serve in the poem? If the lady is trying to distract the man's attention from her body, then the ploy fails spectacularly and she makes little effort to use them in this way. If the comparison is generated by the speaker alone, the result is the same because they appear not to impede his lustful purpose. The more likely point is that in his eager desire, the speaker has confused the significance of the myth (perhaps signalled by his representation of the apples as balls) and has forgotten that the apples/balls do not belong to Atlanta but Aphrodite, the goddess of love. The myth of Atlanta and Hippomenes is not the story of a casual seduction – and such stories are easily found in the *Metamorphoses* – but of a couple who get married. Hippomenes initially scorns the hapless suitors before he is struck by Atlanta's beauty; Atlanta, equally aware of the youth's good looks, initially tries to dissuade him from trying to win her hand because she fears the consequences. More significantly still, the couple's desire for each other leads to their transformation into dangerous beasts, an allegory of the dangers of an excessive trust in the pleasures of sexuality, and a Christian tradition interpreted the myth as a warning of the dangers of succumbing to temptation.[39]

The marriage reference does not mean that the poem has to be redated to fit in with Donne's biography. Rather, it indicates that he was always aware that there was more at stake in sexual relations than simply pleasure, which is why books and reading become prominent in the final section of the elegy, and the speaker's lust is placed in a wider context of thinking about types of love. The speaker reaches for an Ovidian myth that will help to inspire his desire, but finds instead a story of a very different nature, one that reminds readers that sex can be as dangerous as it can be enjoyable, and an all-consuming passion may well prove destructive. Any reader of Ovid's elegies would have known that they become more serious and sad as the speaker realizes that he cannot control the forces he has unleashed. In the following extract from Ovid's Elegies the speaker becomes jealous and tormented as the lovers are at odds:

> Love and hate, here in my heart, at tug of war –
> and love I suppose will find a way to win.
>
> I'd sooner hate. If I can't I'll be the reluctant lover –
> the dumb ox bearing the yoke he loathes.
>
> Your behaviour drives me away, your beauty draws
>   me back.
> I adore your face and abhor your failings.
>
> With or without you life's impossible
> and I can't decide what I want.[40]

Donne's elegy represents a particular moment in the cycle of sexual love. For now, passion, specifically the anticipation of a wonderful sexual encounter, dominates. Of course, as Shakespeare and Nashe remind us, such events can always end in disappointment if desire is not reciprocated and, as in almost all of Donne's poems, we never hear the voice of the woman. His lover is clearly a young man who has much to learn, as he acknowledges, in seeing women as

> Like pictures, or like books' gay coverings made
> For lay-men, are all women thus arrayed;
> Themselves are mystic books, which only we

> Whom their imputed grace will dignify
> Must see revealed. (39–43)

Women may well be disguised, nicely covered up with beautiful clothes, but it is only the lover who will really get to know them properly. At least, that is what the speaker thinks, believing that he will be initiated into the mysteries of the soul when he has sex with a woman. Laymen – that is, those who are not priests of love – can only see the bright covers of books, not having the chance to read their matter.

The analogy might seem persuasive but it opens up the possibility of a deeper, more allegorical reading of the mysteries of sex, suggesting that the physical encounter the speaker is eager to experience may not explain everything that he thinks it will. After all, this is a poem written in anticipation of sex, not during or after the event, and the example of Ovid's elegies would warn even the most callow reader that the mysteries one discovers may not be quite what one expected. The next lines surely undercut the assumptions of the speaker that what the couple will experience is unalloyed pleasure:

> . . . Then, since that I may know,
> As lib'rally as to a midwife, show
> Thyself! Cast all, yea, this white linen hence;
> There is no penance, due to innocence! (43–6)

The white linen may well symbolize the innocence of virginity, but the speaker's confidence that their actions will require no penance is surely misguided (unless they are actually married) because fornication was a sin, as the marriage ceremony in *The Book of Common Prayer* recognized: '[Marriage] was ordained for a remedie against sinne, and to avoid fornication, that suche persones as be married, might live chastlie in matrimonie, and kepe themselves undefiled members of Christes bodye.'[41] The other result of sexual intercourse, as the marriage ceremony also recognized, was 'the procreation of children'. The speaker, undoubtedly without recognizing what he has done, signals this through his demand that the naked woman show herself 'as to a midwife', something she may well have to do later if events take a likely course. If they are married then they are behaving in a perfectly chaste manner, as the *Common Prayer* book recognizes; if they are not, then they may well regret their actions and have to perform penance.

'To His Mistress Going to Bed' is a far more complicated, ambiguous and ironic poem than has often been acknowledged: the lady may well be covered by the man, as the speaker hopes at the end of the poem, but this does not mean that either of them will really understand the mysteries of love. 'The Ecstasy', one of the longest poems in *Songs and Sonnets*, usually thought to be a relatively mature poem and dated as one of the 'marriage poems' (1605–13?), is an equally complicated work that is not quite what it seems to be.[42] Although it has long been recognized as one of Donne's great poems, it has all too often been read as if it were a solemn, philosophical argument, rather than a learned poem written in the light of a number of literary traditions, eager to exploit the poet's erudition in cunning and subtle ways and, as ever, to make a serious point.[43] The title refers to a divine experience when the fortunate individual is transported to a higher plane in order to learn wisdom not normally granted to human beings because it was not accessible via reason and sensory perception. The opening stanza is at odds with the expectations the title has established:

> Where, like a pillow on a bed,
>   A pregnant bank swelled up to rest
> The violet's reclining head,
>   Sat we two, one another's best. (1–4)

These lines probably lead the reader to anticipate that the poem will develop as a pastoral lyric. The lovers are situated in a beautiful, isolated retreat, the familiar *locus amoenus* ('pleasant place') of romance. Hence, after reading the first stanza, we should be aware that all is not quite as it seems, especially if we see any significance in the adjective 'pregnant' (which might draw comparisons with the use of the word 'midwife' in the elegy). This could, of course, simply be a description of the rounded bank. It also, however, reminds us of a state one of the lovers will undoubtedly experience if their romance continues or, as is more likely, may have already experienced if the couple in question are John and Ann Donne.

The pastoral is among the most complex of literary forms. As many Renaissance literary critics noted, the superficial simplicity invariably hid an allegorical message that was at odds with the surface material.[44] Donne rarely employed pastoral forms, his verse being set in London when it had a setting at all, so his use of a bucolic opening here is all the more noteworthy, one designed to emphasize that 'The Ecstasy' should not be taken exactly as it is read. The bizarre imagery of the second stanza, with its complex mixture of quasi-scientific language and images of erotic rapture, bears out such suspicions:

> Our hands were firmly cèmented
> > With a fast balm, which thence did spring;
> Our eye-beams twisted, and did thread
> > Our eyes, upon one double string. (5–8)

The lovers are experiencing a strange encounter that does not obey the normal rules of physical reality. Donne's speaker provides an elaborate description of the pure refinement of the couple's love that allows them to go beyond the constraints of their bodies:

> Our souls, (which to advance their state
> > Were gone out), hung 'twixt her and me.
>
> And whilst our souls negotiate there,
> > We like Sepulchral statues lay;
> All day the same our postures were
> > And we said nothing, all the day.
>
> If any, so by love refined
> > That he soul's language understood,
> And by good love were grown all mind,
> > Within convenient distance stood,
>
> He (though he knew not which soul spake:
> > Because both meant, both spake the same)

Might thence a new concoction take,
> And part far purer than he came. (15–28)

The lovers are united and become one through their perfect
union. They do not even need to speak; so advanced is their
state of love that their souls can communicate, making the
organs of speech redundant. There is a similar moment in
Milton's *Paradise Lost*, Book 8 (published 1667), when Adam
asks Raphael whether angels have sexual intercourse in heaven.
Raphael appears embarrassed, and answers 'with a smile that
glowed / Celestial rosy red, love's proper hue' that the love
of angels goes beyond the physical earthly love that men and
women can experience:

> Whatever pure thou in the body enjoy'st
> (And pure thou wert created) we enjoy
> In eminence, and obstacle find none
> Of membrane, joint, or limb, exclusive bars:
> Easier than air with air, if spirits embrace,
> Total they mix, union of pure with pure
> Desiring; nor need restrained conveyance need
> As flesh to mix with flesh, or soul with soul.[45]

It is quite possible that Donne's poem is a source of
Milton's passage. Milton undoubtedly read Donne and probably heard him preach at St Paul's Cathedral when he was
a child.[46] Raphael explains to Adam that he simply will not
be able to understand how angels behave and that the best
he can provide him with is an approximation of the higher
state that exists nearer God. Donne has his speaker imagine

a hypothetical observer, extensively refined by his own experience of love, who is able to understand their behaviour because he has ceased to be human and has become 'all mind'. This observer will then learn from their example.

The argument of 'The Ecstasy' is cumulative in its depiction of relative states of awareness. The lovers are so far above ordinary mortals that their union will only make sense to a pure being who exists in a more refined state than is possible for humans. The ecstasy they experience moves them up beyond creation and towards the divine love of the angels. Donne is again making use of the popularization of Neoplatonism in the sixteenth century: the lovers will reach a higher plane through the perfection of their mutual love, as celebrated in poems such as Edmund Spenser's *Four Hymns* (1596).[47]

However, just as Donne appears to be celebrating the achievement of his lovers in creating a 'new soul' (line 45), the poem is dramatically transformed. The speaker changes tack and asks why, if their love is so pure and beyond reproach, they neglect their bodies. After all, 'They're ours, though they're not "we", we are / Th'intelligences, they the sphere' (51–2). The lovers cannot be reduced to their bodies because they have gone beyond them to a higher plane, but, just as God takes notice of the lower spheres of creation, so should they make some use of what they have. Their souls will still interact even if the bodies start off the process of intermingling. It may seem demeaning for them to descend to such depths, but it is their sorry duty to have to do so:

T'our bodies turn we, then, that so
    Weak men on love revealed may look:

Love's mysteries in souls do grow,
  But yet the body is his book. (69–72)

This penultimate stanza shows that 'The Ecstasy' is a poem simultaneously enveloped in irony and a serious work of erotic literature, very like the elegy. The use of the adjective 'pregnant' in the poem's second line reminds us that love simply cannot be as ethereal as the speaker claims in the first half of the poem, as we realize towards the end. Donne acknowledges this reality when he compares the body to a book; again, just as he did in the elegy. The language of love has already been written and is surely more complicated and involved than the poetics of Ovidian desire or the language of Neoplatonism if taken in isolation. In a very obvious way the speakers of the elegy and 'The Ecstasy' are right: earthly and spiritual loves need to be combined, but not necessarily quite as they think.

Donne's poems can appear as cynical and dismissive reflections on the nature of love, or as lyrics that claim that love, in moving us beyond the world, means everything. However, neither reading quite explains Donne's explorations of love rooted in the world and building a bridge to the spiritual life. Donne makes use of a series of precursors, styles, types and literary examples, often treating the material at his command in a sardonic or ironic way, only allowing us to equate his voice with those of his speakers in a few poems. Even so, the poems collected as *Songs and Sonnets* make up an extremely serious volume, putting all previous love poetry in its place and declaring that marriage, specifically that of John and Ann Donne, was one of the few constants in a chaotic, untrustworthy and changeable world. In celebrating marriage he was not only following the dominant English poet of the 1590s, Edmund Spenser, who represented marriage as central to his identity as a poet in his work, but exploring the relationship between the demands of living in the world and preparing properly for the afterlife.[48]

Part of the house where Donne lived in Pyrford.

FOUR

Marriage

he decision regarding whether to get married and to whom was far more intricate in early seventeenth-century England than it is in the same country today. In a society in which wealth largely depended on the acquisition of property, good marriage alliances were vital, and most marriages, if not arranged, took place between the offspring of families who knew each other well.[1] Marriage also precluded men from following certain careers, notably, despite the Protestant emphasis on marriage, at the two universities, Oxford and Cambridge, which insisted on the celibacy of dons until the 1860s.[2]

Donne's marriage was, however it is analysed, a spectacular disaster. A particular story, of doubtful authenticity but clearly assumed to represent the truth of the situation, was doing the rounds after the Restoration:

Doctor *Donne* after he was married to a Maid, whose name was *Anne*, in a frolick (on his Wedding day) chalkt on the back-side of his Kitchin-door, *John Donne, Anne Donne, Undone.*[3]

Sr

If a very respective feare of yor displeasure, and a
doubt, that my L: whom I knew owt of yor worthines to loue yᵒᵐ much,
would be so compassionate wᵗʰ yoᵘ, as to adde his anger to yoʳ did not
so much increase my sicknes as that I cannot stirr I had taken the
boldnes to haue donne the office of this letter by wayting vpon yoᵘ
my self. To haue giuen yoᵘ truthe and clearnes of this matter
between yor daughter and me; and to shew to yoᵘ plainly the limitts
of or fault, by wᶜʰ I know yor wisdome wyll proportion the punishmᵗ.
So long since as at her being at yorkhouse this had foundacon: and so
much then of promise and contract built vpon yt as wᵗʰowt violence
to conscience might not be shaken. At her lyeng in town this last
parliamt, I found meanes to see her twice or thrice: we both knew
the obligacons that lay vpon vs, and wee aduentured equally, and about
three weeks before Christmas we married. And as at the doinge, there
were not yet aboue fyue persons, of wᶜʰ I protest to yoᵘ by my saluation
there was not one that had any dependence or relation to yoᵘ: so in all the
passage of it, did I forbear to vse any such person, who by furtherance
of yt might violate any trust or duty towards yoᵘ. The reasons why
I did not forcacquaint yoᵘ wᵗʰ it, (to deale wᵗʰ the same plainnes that I
haue vsd) were these. I knew my present estate lesse then fit for her; I
knew, (yet I knew not why) that I stood not right in yor opinion; I
knew that to haue giuen any intimacon of yt had been to impossibilitate
the whole matter. And then hauing these purposes in or harts and those
fetters in or consciences me thinks we should be pardoned if or fault be but
this, that wee did not by fore-reuealinge of yt consent to or hindrance
and torment. Sr, I acknowledge my fault to be so great, as I dare scarce
offer any other prayer to yoᵘ in myne own behalf, then this to beleeue this
truthe, that I neyther had dishonest end nor meanes. But for her
whom I tender much more then my fortunes, or lyfe (els I would I might
neyther ioy in this lyfe, nor enioy the next) I humbly beg of yoᵘ, that she
may not, to her danger, feele the torror of yor sudaine anger. I know
this letter shall find yoᵘ full of passion: but I know no passion can
alter yor reason and wisdome; to wᶜʰ I aduenture to comend these
particulers; That yt ys irremediably donne; that if yoᵘ incense
my L, yoᵘ destroy her and me; That yt is easye to giue vs happines; And
that my endevors and industrie, if it please yoᵘ to prosper them, may
soone make me somewhat worthyer of her. If any take the

202

John Donne's letter to Sir George More, 2 February 1601/2, where he
relates the circumstances of his marriage to More's daughter Ann and
seeks his favour.

advantage of yo[r] displeasure against me, and fill yo[w] wth ill
thoughts of me, my Comfort is that yo[w] know that fayth and
thanks are due to them onely, that speak when theyr informa-
cions might do good. w[ch] now yt cannot work towards any party.
For my Excuse I can say nothing except I knew what were
sayd to yo[w]. S[r] I have truly told yo[w] this matt[r], and
I humbly beseeche yo[w] so to deale in yt, as the persuasions of
Nature, reason, wisdome, and Christianity shall informe yo[w]
And to accept the vowes of one whom yo[w] may now rayse or
scatter, w[ch] are, that as all my Love ys directed vnchange-
ably vpon her, so all my labors shall concur to her con-
tentment, and show my humble Obedience to yo[r] selfe.

from my Lodginge by [s]r
&uoy: 2° Februa: 1601

yo[rs] in all duty and
humblenes

J: Donne

Two months after his secret marriage Donne confessed what he had done to his father-in-law, Sir George More. The letter, dated 2 February 1602 and delivered by his friend Henry Percy, 9th Earl of Northumberland, who was to intercede for him, indicates that Donne knew that his plea was extremely unlikely to succeed:

> Sir,
> If a very respective fear of your displeasure and a doubt that my Lord [Sir Thomas Egerton] (whom I know, out of your worthiness, to love you very much) would be so compassionate with you as to add his anger to yours did not so much increase my sickness as that I cannot stir, I had taken the boldness to have done the office of this letter by waiting upon you myself to have given you truth and clearness of this matter between your daughter and me, and to show you plainly the limits of our fault, by which I know your wisdom will proportion the punishment . . .
>
> Sir, I have truly told you this matter, and I humbly beseech you so to deal in it as the persuasions of nature, reason, wisdom and Christianity shall inform you, and to accept the vows of one whom you may now raise or scatter – which are, that as my love is directed unchangeably upon her, so all my labours shall concur to her contentment, and to show my humble obedience to yourself.[4]

The letter acknowledges that he is at the mercy of Sir George and is in fear for his future (the illness referred to

may or may not be genuine). Neither the letter nor any
pleading by Northumberland worked: Donne was dismissed
from his post and locked up in the Fleet Prison. Although he
was released two months later, and the validity of the marriage was upheld, he experienced a long period in isolation
and the wilderness before his second career as a clergyman
began well over a decade later. The Donnes spent much of
the next few years scraping a living together as best they could
to support their growing family, dependent on the charity of
friends. In 1602 Ann's cousin, Francis Wolley, allowed the
newly married couple to stay in his house in Pyrford, a village
in Surrey 40 kilometres (25 mi.) – about a day's ride – from
central London.[5]

Dating Donne's poetry is difficult and editors have often
been eager to claim many of his more obviously erotic poems
as early works, mindful of the erotic culture of poetry in the
1590s before the Bishops' Ban (1599), and the general evidence that men tend to write such poetry relatively early in
their lives.[6] There is also the testimony of Sir Richard Baker
(c. 1568–1645), who had known Donne at the Inns of Court.
He was also friendly with Sir Henry Wotton (1568–1639), one
of Donne's closest friends, giving his testimony a particular
value.[7] Baker reports on 'Mr. *John Dunne*, who leaving *Oxford*,
lived at the *Innes of Court*, not dissolute, but very neat; a great
visiter of Ladies, a great frequenter of Playes, a great writer
of conceited Verses.'[8] Baker's account stands in stark contrast
to that of Isaak Walton, Donne's first serious biographer.
Walton had also known Donne as he was vicar of the parish
of St Dunstan-in-the-West, where Donne preached. Walton
would have known Donne only in his last six or seven years,

so his account, which emphasizes the young man's piety, is most likely to have been the version of his youth that Donne wished to present at that stage of his life.[9] Donne himself, in a letter to Sir Robert Ker, Earl of Ancrum (April 1619), accompanying the manuscript of *Biathanatos*, states that 'it is a book written by Jack Donne, and not by Dr. Donne', indicating that the author himself distinguished between his youth and maturity.[10]

In thinking about Donne's representation of love and marriage in his poetry we need to consider what sort of poet he was and how we might read the ways he represents himself, his speakers and the women they address. Donne has been classified as a coterie poet, circulating his work in manuscript form to a close circle of friends (although hardly any holograph manuscripts of his poems survive, manuscripts of his work are still being discovered).[11] Not every writer admired this strategy, with some, like Donne's contemporary Michael Drayton (1563–1631), arguing that 'cabinet' poetry was a dereliction of the poet's duty to reach a wider audience through print. Donne would appear to have been Drayton's primary target:

> Inforcing things in Verse for poesy unfit,
> Mere filthy stuff, that breaks out of the sores of wit:
> What Poet recks the praise upon such antics heap'd,
> Or envies that their lines, in cabinets are kept?
> Though some fantastic fool promote their ragged
>   rhymes,
> And do transcribe them o'er a hundred several
>   times.[12]

Whatever the force of Drayton's objections, his comments demonstrate that poetry written for a select audience can assume a shared knowledge of author and reader that is not available to those outside the circle. The poetry that Drayton admired and aspired to produce looked to poets such as his older contemporary Edmund Spenser, deliberately writing for an audience that would not necessarily know the author, the circle linked together through the medium of print. When we read Donne's poetry now in printed form, the specific nuances of its significance are lost unless we appreciate that it had a different material existence in early modern England to the work of poets like Drayton and Spenser, whose poetry reaches us in exactly the same way.

Donne represents himself in different and varying ways in his poems, which is one of the many reasons why it is so hard to reconstruct his biography from his work. Some, I would like to argue, can be read as versions of his real self, in particular those in which he depicts his marriage, and I will analyse a number of these in this chapter. Others represent a more problematic figure who may or may not be a version of Donne. There is, of course, the possibility of overlap and of error in identifying which poems belong to which category, but the distinction surely holds true and serves as a means of categorizing his lyric poetry.

'The Flea' was one of Donne's most popular poems and was published as the opening work in the second edition of his poems (1635).[13] It was much imitated by contemporary poets, and is often dated to the early 1590s, in line with Sir Richard Baker's account of Donne's time at the Inns of Court, the flea biting two lovers so that their blood mingles having a long history in erotic verse.[14] 'The Flea' is often taken to be Donne's most characteristic poem, an example of the lecherous and witty young Jack Donne at his most rampant.[15] However, the voice in the poem is perhaps more subtle, witty and personal than has often been realized, which suggests that it was written after rather than before his marriage to Ann.

The poem begins dramatically, like many of Donne's lyrics, *in medias res*, forcing the reader to reconstruct the encounter and imagine how the couple came to be in a room together: 'Mark but this flea, and mark in this / How little that which thou deny'st me is' (lines 1–2). These opening lines make the situation clear enough. The speaker is a man who wishes to persuade a reluctant woman, who has already rebuffed his advances, to go to bed with him. He uses the example of the flea to show her that surrendering her honour to him is not of great consequence, so she might as well submit and enjoy the experience, a familiar male strategy in early modern poetry. The three stanzas of the poem reveal the speaker using a variety of strategies in response to dramatic developments in the situation. In the first stanza he claims that the insect has sucked the blood of both of them, so he argues that mingling their bodily fluids through sexual intercourse is of no greater consequence. In the second she has obviously threatened to kill the flea, so he counters that the flea represents their marriage: therefore, killing it would be a sacrilege. In the final stanza she has killed the flea, so he argues that as its death has caused no serious consequences, neither will their making love.

Not only were such seduction poems so common that they formed a recognizable type of literature, but the 'flea' poem

formed a distinct sub-genre within this larger group. As
Murray Roston has pointed out, because Ovid was thought
to be the author of an erotic 'flea' poem, imitations and adaptations were so numerous that an anthology of them was
compiled in France in 1582.[16] Donne's poem therefore follows the norms and traditions of classical erotic poetry and
its later European forms, and should not be read as a scan-
dalous and challenging confrontational work because of its
subject matter and approach to sexual relations. It is the
second stanza, I think, that makes the lyric both interesting
and distinctive:

> Oh stay! Three lives in one flea spare
> Where we almost – nay more than – married are:
>   This flea is you and I, and this
> Our marriage-bed, and marriage-temple is.
>   Though parents grudge, and you, we're met,
> And cloistered in these living walls of jet.
>   Though use make thee apt to kill me,
> Let not to this, self-murder added be,
> And sacrilege – three sins in killing three. (10–18)

The second line has invariably been taken as a metaphor, with
the poet addressing an unnamed lady – real or fictional – as
though she were his wife simply as a means of gratifying his
appetites.[17] But it is surely more plausible to read this lyric as
a witty marriage poem, one addressed by a fictionalized
Donne to Ann. The wit of the first four lines works best if
we imagine that the speaker is addressing someone to whom
he is not just pretending to be married, but is actually married.

What seems like a hypothesis is, in fact, true. Donne uses a similar device when his speaker addresses God in Divine Meditation 11, a sonnet that also depends on the interplay between the fictional and the real.[18]

The lines 'This flea is you and I, and this / Our marriage-bed, and marriage-temple is,' would appear to refer to the poverty that the Donnes had to endure together. If so, then Donne has adapted a prominent form of the seduction poem as a humorous and witty comment on his own fate – as well as that of the wife he also ruined. The reason why the lady will not be shamed by surrendering to him is because, so the speaker assumes, there is nothing wrong with a husband and wife making love. Even more to the point, perhaps, their marriage has already brought them a great deal of poverty and shame, so advertising their love life will probably not make a lot of difference to their reputation (and the poem only circulated in manuscript after Donne's death). Donne refers to the 'parents' grudge', surely signalling Sir George More's objection to the marriage, which never really abated.

The description of the lovers 'cloistered in these living walls of jet' is one of many images in Donne's poems of small rooms as an escape from a hostile world: again, the reader might infer that this powerful image could well refer to Donne's own life. The lovers are like monks or nuns cut off from the world (perhaps in Pyrford?), cloistered in their cell together. The walls, made of expensive black marble (jet), hem them in as though they were a further hostile force keeping them there so that the riches of their dwelling further remind them that they are deprived of their freedom (and does the black suggest a womb-like space?). The last line of the stanza, indicating that the lady will commit 'three sins in killing three' could be taken to refer to her pregnancy (the result of their bodily fluids mingling as they do in the flea) and the need for the couple to make the best of their circumstances when they can do little to change them. The Donnes produced a child each year they stayed in Pyrford, further circumstantial evidence that the poem might well date from their time there.

If this conjecture is correct, then 'The Flea' might well be read as a companion piece to 'The Sun Rising', a poem that can definitely be dated to the early 1600s (after 1603 and the accession of James I) and so was almost certainly written during Donne's stay at Pyrford. As in 'The Flea', Donne provides a variation on a well-known and traditional form of lyric. Here, he adapts the poem of the lover addressing the dawn after a night spent with his mistress (the alba or aubade), having his speaker curse the sun with considerable venom rather than simply regret parting from his lover as the day dawns. Ovid, one of the principal influences on the young Donne, had the speaker in his *Amores* long for the pleasures afforded by the night:

> Here she comes, over the sea from her poor
>   husband,
> frosty axle turning, bringing the yellow day.
>
> Why hurry, Aurora? Hold your horses, for
>   Memmon's sake
> and the annual sacrifice of his birds.

Now's the time when I love to lie in my love's soft
 arms,
the time of times to feel her body close to mine.

The time when sleep is heavy, the air is cold,
and birdsong sweetest.

Why hurry? Lovers hate your company.
Tighten the reins in your rosy fingers.

Before coming sailors can better watch their
 stars
and keep their course in open waters.

Travellers however tired rise when you appear
and soldiers reach for their weapons.

Your eye first lights on peasants shouldering
 their mattocks [hoes]
and drags oxen under the yoke.

You rob children of sleep, condemn them
to classrooms and the cruel cane.[19]

Ovid's narrator articulates a weary contempt for the dawn,
providing a long list of supposedly undesirable diurnal events
that he knows, as the reader does, will all happen anyway. The
poem is characterized by wry regret that the pleasures of love
cannot last forever because time hastens on, linking the lyric
to the *carpe diem* ('seize the day') motif prevalent in classical

and European poetry.[20] Ovid's poem serves as a frustrated
and absurd lament for what cannot be.

'The Sun Rising' presents us with the same situation,
represented in a different way. As in 'The Flea' the opening
lines signal the generic conventions: 'Busy old fool, unruly
Sun, / Why dost thou thus / Through windows and through
curtains call on us? / Must to thy motions lovers' seasons
run?' (lines 1–4). Donne employs the familiar staged argument whereby the male lover demonstrates that he is at odds
with reality, but whereas Ovid provides a series of futile obser-
vations, Donne demands that the rhythms of the natural
world obey the dictates of his desires:

> Saucy pedantic wretch! Go chide
> Late schoolboys, and sour prentices;
> Go tell Court-huntsmen, that the King will ride;
> Call country ants to harvest offices:
> Love, all alike, no season knows, nor clime,
> Nor hours, days, months, which are the rags of time
> (5–10)

This complex and startling passage juxtaposes a number
of ideas and contexts. Like so many of Donne's poems it
demands to be read in terms of a commonly known history
of poetry; a current historical situation; intellectual currents
operating in the Renaissance; and, most importantly, his own
life. Unless we take some or all of these factors into account
we will surely miss the subtle ironies of the stanza.

The lover addresses the sun in irreverent terms as a 'saucy
pedantic wretch', imagining that the sun had a choice whether

to rise or not and is simply behaving outrageously badly in shining so early. Clearly such words place the reader at odds with the speaker, exposing him as a victim of the madness that afflicts those passionately in love, while the reader stands as part of the ordinary world against which he rails. But, as was generally assumed in Donne's day, the mad would often alternate between speaking nonsense and speaking the truth that no one else dared to say.[21] The following two lines, as has often been noted, are a swipe at the behaviour of King James, and his addiction to hunting at the expense of governing the kingdom he claimed he wanted to rule so badly, an obsession that shocked his English subjects after he assumed the throne as it interfered with his ability to govern effectively.[22] James and his courtiers are equated with schoolboys and irritable apprentices, suggesting that they all perform equally minor tasks, peripheral to the serious business of life. On the one hand, this shows the conceit of the myopic lover; on the other, it suggests how petty public life in England had become. Love may well know no days or seasons, but then neither do those who choose to go out hunting instead of ruling the kingdom. And, if the lover is a figure of Donne himself, then his marriage to Ann More left him with a great deal of time on his hands to contemplate such matters. Donne may well be reflecting that, unlike the king, who was eager to go out hunting, he had no real need to get out of bed in the morning, so had good reason to curse the sun.

As the short narrative continues, the ego of the lover reaches ever greater proportions. In the second stanza the speaker imagines the lovers leaving their bed behind so that they can block out the world: 'Thy beams so reverend and

strong / Why shouldst thou think? / I could eclipse and cloud
them with a wink, / But that I would not lose her sight so
long' (11–14). The exaggerated compliment to the woman is
made partly as a means of exploding the Petrarchan tradition
in English poetry, whereby the lover heaped praise upon a
silent and impossibly beautiful lady.[23] Sir Philip Sidney, in his
sonnet sequence *Astrophil and Stella* (early 1580s), had already
made this tradition complicated and at least partially ironic
in having Astrophil praise Stella in absurdly artificial terms
(Sonnet 9) and confuse himself with ridiculous twists of
grammar (Sonnet 63) before she explicitly rejects him (Ninth
Song).[24]

Donne makes the reader aware that he can do what he
likes in his paper world, unlike the real one where his status
has been reduced to that of a supplicant desperate, like so
many, for the bounty of a patron. The lover's celebration of
his angry power stands in stark contrast to his situation in
the real world outside the poem, as the references to the king
and the court make clear. The speaker appears to make the
woman all-powerful. He could eclipse the world by closing
his eyes, but her eyes are so stunningly beautiful that they
outshine the sun: 'If her eyes have not blinded thine, / Look,
and tomorrow (late) tell me, / Whether both Indias of spice
and mine / Be where thou left'st them or lie here with me'
(15–18). Petrarchan ladies were usually compared to and
associated with precious stones and exotic jewels, so the exaggerated compliment makes the speaker's lover even more
fabulous and beautiful than any of them.[25] However, in seem-
ing to grant the woman extraordinary powers, he is also
constructing her as his partner in poverty, complicit in the

fantasy world the poem creates to compensate for their lack of agency in the real one. Here, the two outcasts are equated with the highest offices in the land: he can eclipse the sun, she outshines it, mimicking the exaggerated compliments paid to rulers.[26] The subtext of the poem is that they must make their love potent together because they have no choice, as it is all they have.

The second stanza ends with the whole world moving into their bed: 'Ask for those Kings whom thou saw'st yesterday, / And thou shalt hear, "All here in one bed lay"' (19–20). The final stanza continues this line of rhetorical exaggeration, confirming the lovers' centrality:

> She's all states, and all princes, I;
>   Nothing else is.
> Princes do but play us: compared to this,
> All honour's mimic, all wealth alchemy.
>   Thou, Sun, art half as happy as we
>   In that the world's contracted thus:
> Thine age asks ease, and since thy duties be
> To warm the world, that's done in warming us.
> Shine here to us, and thou art everywhere:
> This bed thy centre is, these walls, thy sphere.
>   (21–30)

Having asserted that all kings exist within their bed, so inviting the supposedly assembled monarchs into the chamber, the lover now banishes them. The change in focus and argument resembles the sudden shift in argument at the end of 'The Flea', another personal poem set in a small room. The lovers now blot out the world outside rather than stand for the whole. 'Princes do but play us' suggests that the lover is now asserting that they are the equal of or superior to kings in significance. Rather, they live a life that is more fulfilling, as the subsequent references to honour and wealth in the following line indicate. Again, if this is about Donne's own situation, the irony is especially pointed, given that his marriage left him without a job or prospects, publicly shamed by his father-in-law and penniless. In Ovid's poem the lover wishes the night to continue and curses the dawn because he wants to spend longer in the arms of his beloved; in Donne's poem there is no other world for him and the break of day cruelly reminds him that there is one for others.

The final lines reaffirm the sense of mutual dependence that the lovers have been forced to adopt, that they can only exist in each other, so at odds are they with the world outside their little room. The world has indeed contracted and they will have to accept this as a *fait accompli*. In the fictional world of the poem they can at least make the sun shine for them and control his power. Donne's lover speaks and the lady remains silent, the traditional relationship between the sexes in erotic poetry that women poets such as Mary Wroth sought to confront in her sonnet sequence *Pamphilia to Amphilanthus* (published 1621), which has each lover addressing the other. On this score Donne remains a deeply conservative poet, with the prominent exception of the elegy 'Sappho to Philaenis'.[27] Nevertheless, poems such as 'The Flea' and 'The Sun Rising' demonstrate that Donne not only was acutely aware of the different subject positions he adopted in his poetry and the problematic power relationship between men and women, but he used autobiographical material to affirm a more balanced and mutual relationship between himself and his wife. Of course, the achievement has come partly as a result of failure to achieve worldly success, an irony that could hardly have escaped Donne. And, given the dominant monological power of Donne's poetic voice, the poems hardly reveal an obvious parity.

Another celebrated poem that appears to belong to this group written in the early 1600s is 'The Canonization'. The title, in both contemporary manuscripts and the first edition of Donne's poems, would appear to be authorial and in common use.[28] Like 'The Relic', the poem makes an explicit comparison between the love of the couple and religious, specifically Catholic, sanctification. The poem may well have been occasioned by a letter from his friend Tobie Matthew (1577–1655), who had criticized Donne for failing to attend court as part of his professional duties.[29] Matthew converted to Catholicism soon after he travelled to Italy in 1604, so the title may contrast the proper love of the Donnes with Matthew's betrayal of his country. The opening lines of Donne's poem are voiced, yet again, with the strident and confrontational declaration of his love:

> For God's sake hold your tongue, and let me love!
> > Or chide my palsy, or my gout;
> My five grey hairs, or ruined fortune flout;
> With wealth your state, your mind with arts improve,
> > Take you a course, get you a place,
> > Observe his Honour, or his Grace,
> And the King's real, or his stampèd face

Contèmplate: what you will, approve,
  So you will let me love. (1–9)

Yet again, Donne draws the reader's attention to his worldly
failures, his ageing (the grey hairs indicate that he is in his
thirties, exactly Donne's age in the 1600s) and the ruin of
his once-anticipated fortune. The stanza contrasts the desire
for success of the addressee, his unnamed friend, with his
own commitment to love. The friend, who, like the women
in Donne's poems, never speaks, balances his pursuit of afflu-
ence with the desire to improve himself through education
(line 4), the heavy caesura implying that the two are intimately connected for those who follow the ways of the world
rather than the path of love. The friend can pursue whatever
project he likes, obtain any position in a noble household
('Honour') or with a high-ranking cleric ('Grace'), and either
serve the king at court, or accumulate piles of objects with
his image on it ('his stampèd face' referring to coins), so long
as he leaves the speaker alone.

We cannot take the poem at face value. It articulates exactly
what Donne has lost through his improvident marriage, and
what he appears to have wanted before he lost it all. In Donne's
day recent literary history was littered with examples of
sophisticated, worldly poets pretending to have rejected what
they really wanted. An earlier poet whose work, like Donne's,
circulated in manuscript before it was published, had made
an identical manoeuvre, based on the rhetorical trope *occu-
patio*, or highlighting what the author claims he or she is
denying.[30] Sir Philip Sidney claimed, in Sonnet 30 of *Astrophil
and Stella*, that his love for Stella (Penelope Devereux, to whom

the young Sidney was betrothed before the engagement was broken off) obliterated his interest in politics:

Whether the Turkish new-moone minded be
To fill his hornes this yeare on Christian coast;
How *Poles'* right king meanes, without leave of hoast,
To warme with ill-made fire cold *Moscovy*:
If French can yet three parts in one agree;
What now the Dutch in their full diets boast;
How *Holland* hearts, now so good townes be lost,
Trust in the shade of pleasing *Orange* tree;
How *Ulster* likes of that same golden bit,
Wherewith my father once made it halfe tame;
If in the Scottishe Court be weltring yet;
These questions busie wits to me do frame;
I, cumbered with good maners, answer do,
But know not how, for still I thinke of you.[31]

Those who knew anything about Sidney would realize that he had a particular interest in European politics and that when he answers questions, as if politely because he is thinking of Stella, he does so with impressive knowledge. Indeed, the declaration throughout the sonnet that he knows nothing about Turkey, Poland, Russia, France, Holland, Ireland and Scotland carefully demonstrates just how much he knows about current affairs, a joke that a coterie audience would have understood.

The same, of course, might be said of Donne's marriage, and 'The Canonization' provides enough clues for us to be able to separate it from what look like earlier poems that reflect more generally on erotic encounters. The second stanza wittily exposes the speaker, making it obvious that he is a slightly absurd version of Donne himself. It opens 'Alas, alas! Who's injured by my love?' (line 10) before providing a list of people and things that will not have been affected by whomever the speaker loves, and whatever he has done: merchants' ships will still sail, his tears do not flood parks and pastures, his colds do not 'a forward spring remove' (13), his hot blood does not cause plagues, soldiers are still able to fight wars and lawyers are not prevented from finding litigious quarrels. Enmeshed within the generic descriptions of Jacobean activity are some specific references to Donne himself and the Donnes. The forceful rhetorical question in the first line rebounds on the speaker as the people most hurt by the Donnes' clandestine marriage were, of course, the Donnes themselves. There is also surely a joke about Donne's own notorious bad health — why he knew so much about medicine — in the comments about his colds and his hot blood, which does not cause plague.[32]

The poem continues to establish an ironic distance between the poet and the speaker, making it, like so many of Donne's lyrics, a dramatic monologue. As in 'The Flea', the interlocutor clearly speaks at some point but their voice remains deliberately silenced. Stanza three charges him (the poem would appear to indicate that the other figure is male) to 'Call us what you will' (19), forcing the reader to imagine what has been said (seducer? harlot? fornicators?), unless the following line provides a clue ('Call her one, me another fly' (20)), which suggests that the couple may have been referred to as flies, disgusting insects that breed ceaselessly and thoughtlessly.[33] In countering that they are actually the eagle and the dove (22) Donne jokes about the common perception of the nature of their marriage, that he was a predatory seducer and she a passive dove.[34]

The next lines, comparing their love to the riddle of the phoenix, assert that such close relationships are private and therefore beyond the comprehension of even intimate friends and close acquaintances. There is a subtle and humorous allusion to their sexuality:

> So to one neutral thing both sexes fit,
>   We die and rise the same and prove
>   Mysterious by this love. (25–7)

While the first line cited here represents the couple as a hermaphrodite, the second makes an obvious pun on orgasm ('die') and erection ('rise'), together ('die and rise') reproducing the movement of copulation and so undermining the apparent neutrality of the sexes joined together in re-establishing the sexual nature of their relationship. The lines may refer to Donne's earlier poetry and reputation, and they also wittily breathe new life into the cliché that love is a mystery.[35] On the one hand, it is, and every couple is unique and unknowable; on the other, the dance and language of love remain more or less the same.

The penultimate stanza continues the sexual theme, but immediately transforms it into a poetic analysis of poetry:

> We can die by it, if not live by love,
>   And if unfit for tombs or hearse

Our legend be, it will be fit for verse;
And if no piece of chronicle we prove,
    We'll build in sonnets pretty rooms –
    As well a well-wrought urn becomes
The greatest ashes, as half-acre tombs –
    And by these hymns, all shall approve
    Us canonized for Love. (28–36)

Their love may be unsuitable for recording in funeral mon-
uments (because it is too bawdy? too secret? too ordinary?),
but it can be recorded in verse. In itself this is a tantalizing
hint: is that because their love resembles that represented in
Donne's earlier poetry? Or because it is different? The Donnes
may not be the subject of a history, because they are not significant or important in worldly terms, but their love will
prove important because it will be recorded in poetry, which
will provide a fitting memorial or monument. Yet again there
is a reminder of their reduced circumstances: they will build
sonnets in 'pretty rooms' that will stand in stark contrast to
the enclosed spaces they have been forced to inhabit, and
because, apart from making love, there is little else to do. The
memorable phrase 'a well-wrought urn' has indeed proved
Donne right, as it has served as an example of his poetic wit
and devotion to his spouse, canonizing him as a poet.[36]

Although some have doubted whether 'A Nocturnal upon
St Lucy's Day' was written after the death of Ann on 15
August 1617, five days after giving birth to a still-born child,
it is hard not to read this poem in terms of the earlier works
that expressed the speaker's devotion to his spouse.[37] There
is the same strand of alchemical imagery running throughout

the work as there is in the poems that appear to celebrate his
love when he was first married, and the overwrought description of his desire for destruction inverts the imagery of
inseparable union in those earlier marriage poems:

> All others, from all things draw all that's good –
> Life, soul, form, spirit – whence they being have;
>   I, by Love's limbeck, am the grave
>   Of all: that's nothing. Oft a flood
>   Have we two wept, and so
> Drowned the whole world, us two; oft did we grow
> To be two Chaoses, when we did show
> Care to aught else; and often absences
> Withdrew our souls, and made us carcasses.
>
> But I am by her death (which word wrongs her)
> Of the first nothing the elixir grown.
>   Were I a man, that I were one
>   I needs must know; I should prefer,
>   If I were any beast,
> Some ends, some means; yea, plants – yea stones
>   – detest
> And love: all, all some properties invest.
> If I an ordinary nothing were,
> As shadow, a light and body must be here. (19–36)

Donne imagines himself as the quintessence of nothing,
merging the language of alchemy ('limbeck', 'chaos', 'souls',
'elixir', 'shadow') and the theology of his Holy Sonnets, with
their emphasis on the desire for annihilation.[38] The image

of weeping also seems to refer to earlier marriage poems, 'The Canonization' and, more significantly, 'A Valediction of Weeping', perhaps written when Donne travelled to France and Italy in 1605.[39] In that poem the copious tears of the lovers create a world that unites them because they 'are nothing' when 'on a diverse shore' (line 9) and together they form the oceans that connect everything that exists: 'thy tears mixed with mine do overflow / This world, by waters sent from thee, my Heav'n, dissolvèd so' (16–17).

The images in 'A Nocturnal' are diametrically opposed to those in 'A Valediction', with everything now pointing towards death rather than life. The speaker, who bears a striking resemblance to the real Donne, imagines himself, as he does in his sermons and religious poems, as the quintessence of death, the negation of matter and animated life, 'the grave / Of all: that's nothing', an ambiguous pairing of phrases with complicated syntax despite the use of demotic vocabulary. The lines express both an apparent despair and the theological conundrum of how we can imagine 'nothing' in a universe in which God has created everything.[40] The poet is acutely aware of the fine dividing line between substance and nothing, how the body has no significance without the soul that animates it. 'Chaos' was the contemporary name for unformed matter that had yet to be given proper life by a presiding deity and Donne describes the lovers as two 'chaoses' – which is, of course, impossible – when they engage with the world outside themselves and so disrupt their own harmony. The reference would appear to be to the emphasis in Donne's earlier poems on the couple's mutual dependence counteracting the hostility and indifference of the world

outside. Separation always threatened to transform the couple into inanimate carcasses, and now they have to face the reality of the words of the marriage ceremony in *The Book of Common Prayer*, that they will be united until 'death us departe'.[41] The speaker feels that his partner's death has rendered him less than primeval chaos, the very absence of

Unknown artist, *Henry King, Bishop of Chichester*, n.d., oil on canvas.

creation, and he attempts to express his sense of loss through an understanding that he cannot imagine that his body has any properties at all, though it must at least cast a shadow.

'A Nocturnal' can be compared with the lament of Bishop Henry King (1592–1669); for his wife, also called Anne, who died aged 24 in 1624.[42] King was a close friend of Donne, and the two men were intimately associated. He clearly knew Donne's poems and sermons well, and often made use of them in his own writing. He was one of Donne's executors, commissioned the statue of him in St Paul's Cathedral and may well have edited the edition of Donne's poems published in 1633.[43] It is likely that his own reflections on painful bereavement look back to those of Donne. 'The Exequy' contains a sustained passage on the significance of weeping, time and an obliviousness to the world:

> . . . For thee (lov'd clay)
> I languish out not live, the day,
> Using no other exercise
> But what I practise with mine eyes:
> By which wet glasses I find out
> How lazily time creeps about
> To one that mourns: this, onely this,
> My exercise and bus'ness is.
> So I compute the weary hours
> With sighs dissolved into showres.
>
> Nor wonder if my time go thus
> Backward and most preposterous;
> Thou hast benighted me, thy set

This Eve of blackness did beget,
Who was't my day, (though overcast
Before thou had'st thy noon-tide past)
And I remember must in tears,
Thou scarce had'st seen so many years
As Day tells houres.[44]

As in 'A Nocturnal', King is acutely aware of the delicate
division between life and death, and that bodies revert to
their natural substance (clay) after a pitifully short time.
Donne laments the shortest day when daylight hours turn
most rapidly into night; King also meditates upon time, diurnal divisions and light and darkness, concluding that his wife's
death has inaugurated an 'Eve of blackness' and that for him
the light no longer shines as it once did. Donne's recollection
of weeping when parting and then grieving would seem to be
refigured by King as he spends the days crying for his loss,
finding it the only way that he can link himself to her now
that she is dead. Just as Donne found that he was made into
something even less than nothing by Ann's death, so does
King discover that time has no meaning for him any more
and so he desires to go backwards to the time when she was
still alive. Even then the divisions of the day only serve to
remind him that she lived only for as many years as there are
hours in the day.

The conclusion of 'The Exequy' makes explicit what is
implicit in 'A Nocturnal' but which is a central assumption
of virtually all Donne's writing: only through death can the
lovers be reunited and the soul reanimated:

> . . . *Dear* (forgive
> The crime) I am content to live
> Divided, with but half a heart,
> Till we shall meet and never part. (117–20)

Donne's poem concludes with an image of the black sun, a common representation of depression.[45] In the bitterness of his loss he dismisses other lovers as merely lecherous through the depiction of the lustful goat used also in the Holy Sonnets, as he imagines his body having no substance and leaving no shadow:

> But I am none; nor will my sun renew.
> You lovers, for whose sake the lesser Sun
>   At this time to the Goat is run
>   To fetch new lust, and give it you,
>   Enjoy your summer all:
> Since she enjoys her long night's festival,
> Let me prepare t'wards her, and let me call
> This hour her vigil, and her eve, since this
> Both the year's, and the day's deep midnight is.
> (37–45)[46]

The emphasis on the issue of 'nothingness', and the distinction between animated matter, death and the union of souls, indicate that this poem makes sense only in terms of Donne's representation of his relationship with his wife elsewhere. The words 'Let me prepare t'wards her' – especially if they are recalled in King's description of having to live with half a heart until he dies and is reunited with his Anne

Annæ

Georgij
Roberti
Willelmi   { More de   { Filiæ
Christophori   Lothesley   Soror:
                Equit: Nept:
                Aurat: pronepti:

Fœmina Lectissimæ, Dilectissimæqᵉ;
Coniugi charissimæ castissimæqᵉ;
Matri piissima, & Dulgentissimæqᵉ;
XV annis in coniugio transactis,
vii post xiiᵐ partum (quorum vii superstant) dies
          Annani febre correpta,
(Quod hoc saxum farj iussit
     Ipse, præ dolore Infans)
Maritus (miserrimum dictu) olim chara charus
Cineribus cineres spondet suos

Nouo matrimonio (annuat Deus) hoc loco sociandos,
          Johannes   Donne
          Sacr: Theolog: profess:
              Secessit
Aᵒ xxxiiiᵒ Ætatis suæ et sui Jesu.
      (1) D C Xviiᵒ
          Aug: xv.

129

Epitaph on Ann dau: of Sr Geo. More
wife of Dr John Donne

she died 15 Augt 1617 aged 33
had been married 15 years
1602

– suggest that the only way to live is to think about death,
when his body will be reunited with his soul and his soul will
be reunited with that of Ann.

Donne wrote a Latin epitaph for his wife dated 15 August
1617, designed for her tombstone. The tomb has been destroyed
but the epitaph survives in a number of versions in manuscripts.[47] Donne expresses his love for his wife and his hope
for their reunion – just as King does in his poem – and for
a public monument as a permanent record:

> *Faeminae Lectissimae, dilectissimaeque;*
> *Conjiugi charissimae, castissimaeque;*
> *Matri piissimae, Indulgentissimaeque;*
> *XV annis in conjugio transactis,*
> *VII post XII Partum (quorum superstant) dies*
> *Immani fibre correptae,*
> *(quod hoc saxum fari jussit*
> *Ipse, prae dolore Infans)*
> *Maritus (miserrimum dictu) olim charae charus*
> *Cineribus cineres spondet suos*
> *Novo matrimonio (annuat Deus) hoc loco sociandos*

> A woman most choice or select/read, most beloved/
>   loving/well-read,
> A spouse most dear, most chaste,
> A mother most loving/merciful/pious/dutiful, most
>   self-sacrificing/indulgent;
> Fifteen years in union/covenant completed,
> Seven days after the twelfth parturition (of whom
>   seven survive)

By a savage/immense/ravishing fever hurriedly
    carried off/seized
(Wherefore this stone to speak he commanded
Himself by/beyond grief [made] speechless [Infant/
    infant])
Her husband (most miserable/wretched to say/
    designation/assertion) once
dear to the dear
His own ashes to these ashes pledges [weds]
[in a] New marriage (may God assent) in this place
    joining together[48]

FIVE

Learning

I

n his search for poetic inspiration, Donne seems
to have paid close attention to two distinct, albeit
interrelated, bodies of poetry: the works produced
in the years after the end of the Roman Republic and the
establishment of the empire, and the poetry written by his
immediate contemporaries in London. In doing so he styles
himself as a metropolitan poet, making a link between the
greatest city of the ancient world on the cusp of its expansion
and assumption of world domination, and a similar situation
in contemporary England. Donne was not only a poet who
was theologically literate and learned, but was heavily invested
in the history of poetry (and the literature of ancient Rome
in particular), European letters and current trends and
fashions in English literature.[1]

Donne was, of course, hardly alone in demonstrating
enthusiasm for such poets as Ovid, Catullus, Martial and
Juvenal, or in trying to adapt and imitate their writings.
Marlowe and Shakespeare, as already noted, wrote a great
deal of Ovidian verse at the start of their writing careers, and
Shakespeare also chose to narrate the foundation of the
Roman Republic in *The Rape of Lucrece*. When Ben Jonson

collected his poems together in the ground-breaking folio
edition of his *Works* in 1616, he included a complete book of
epigrams in imitation of Martial, and a number of poems in
The Forest and *The Underwood* that were adaptations and imitations of Catullus' lyrics. So many poets published aggressive
satires in the style of Juvenal in the 1590s that they were
eventually banned in 1599.[2] Donne's work emerges as part of
the creative ferment of late Elizabethan England, which had
as one of its principal coordinates the poetry of Julio-Claudian
Rome, a busy city at the heart of the world with its cultural
magnificence, prominent citizens leading important lives,
erotic and political intrigue, and endemic corruption. Donne
represents his own life in his poetry in terms that resemble
those of his Roman forebears.

Donne's classicism is in striking contrast to that of Ben
Jonson, generally considered the English Renaissance poet
who most desired to imitate a Latin style of writing.[3] Jonson
attempts to forge a plain and clear style in his work that will
survive as long after his death as that of the poets of
Augustan Rome. He makes every effort to write about types
and situations that have a universal relevance beyond the
moment of their inception. Jonson's song 'To Celia' has as
its literary predecessor Catullus' poem to Lesbia. Where
Catullus has 'We should live, my Lesbia, and love / And value
all the talk of stricter / Old men at a single penny' (5, lines
1–3), Jonson adapts in his translation to 'Come, my Celia, let
us prove, / While we may, the sports of love; / Time will not
be ours for ever; / He, at length, our good will sever.'[4] The
theme is the familiar one of *carpe diem*, the need to act quickly
before time rushes away (the song was originally sung by the

eponymous protagonist of Jonson's play *Volpone*). However, in pointed contrast, Jonson's poetic language is designed to last, to create a literary work that will be comprehensible to future generations, moving beyond its immediate moment.

When Jonson writes on the death of his first daughter, he adapts Martial's lament for the death of his slave girl Erotion, ending his poem with the couplet, 'This grave partakes the fleshy birth; / Which cover lightly, gentle earth.' Martial concludes his with the lines, 'Lie lightly on her, turf and dew: / She put so little weight on you' (Book 5, Epigram 34).[5] The sincerity of both versions of the elegy exists in the attempt to construct a funeral monument in verse that future generations will be able to read. Indeed, the next epigram in Jonson's verse collection is dedicated to Donne, whom he knew well (Donne contributed dedicatory verses to *Volpone* in 1607). In praising Donne sincerely, Jonson acknowledges their differences:

> Donne, the delight of Phoebus and each Muse,
> > Who, to thy one, all other brains refuse;
> Whose every work of thy most early wit
> > Came forth example, and remains so yet:
> Longer a-knowing than most wits do live,
> > And which no affection praise enough can give!
> To it, thy language, letters, arts, best life,
> > Which might with half mankind maintain a strife.
> All which I meant to praise, and yet I would,
> > But leave, because I cannot as I should![6]

Amid the praise it is hard not to hear some criticism in the point that Donne has lived rather longer than most wits, and in the author's admission that he cannot praise Donne as he would like to. They are, as Jonson recognizes, dissimilar poets.

Donne adopts different strategies to Jonson in his poetry, as is apparent from his attempts to capture the immediacy of Ovid's poems of frantic lust and of Juvenal's patrician scorn for the dirt and squalor of the city. When Donne uses a theme familiar from Latin poetry he emphasizes its urgent significance as a motif spoken by a lover in the heat of the moment or a disaffected and sardonic wit incredulous at the incompetence and mendacity he sees around him. Donne's satires have a relationship to Juvenal similar to that of many of his erotic poems to Ovid. Juvenal (1st–2nd century CE), about whom little is known, was invariably seen as an aggressive and hostile satirist, at odds with the world and eager to point out its flaws rather than correct them. His work stands in contrast to the satires of Horace (65–8 BCE), which are much gentler and more instructive, designed to correct the faults observed in the poems.[7] Juvenal's satires are an acknowledgement of the triumph of Rome as the world's first city. He rails against vice that he believes cannot be removed, only avoided. Juvenal has no real desire to leave Rome behind and seek a more temperate life in the provinces: his literary persona may well claim that he wants to do this but the reader understands that he is not being entirely honest. When he opens the second satire with the wish that he might escape 'Northward beyond the Lapps to the world's end, the frozen / Polar ice-cap', because he has been forced to listen to 'Highflown moral discourse from that clique in Rome who affect / Ancestral peasant virtues as a front for their lechery', we know that he is only indulging in rhetorical excess.[8] Rome is morally flawed because it has been so successful, triumphing over all its enemies and dominating the known world, which means that it contains a multitude of forms of life, both good and bad. Accordingly, the satirist and the object of his satire live side by side and exist in a symbiotic relationship.

Juvenal's first satire has the unfortunate poet forced to listen to dreadful poetry readings, and wishing that he could exact his revenge on the talentless bore who is droning away in front of the audience:

> Must I *always* be stuck in the audience at these poetry
>   readings,
> never on the platform myself, taking it out on Cordus
> For the times he's bored me to death with ranting
>   speeches
> From that *Thesiad* of his? Is X to get off scot-free
> After inflicting his farces on me, or Y his elegies?
>   Is there
> No recompense for whole days wasted on prolix
> Versions of *Telephus?* (1–7)

The satirist's instinct is to retreat into a private world away from the awfulness of life lived in public spaces. Donne's first satire has a similar opening, as his speaker desires to be left alone with his books and to escape from the superficial courtier who insists on shadowing him. Donne makes it clear where his priorities should lie:

> Away thou changeling motley humorist!
> Leave me, and in this standing wooden chest,

Consorted with these few books, let me lie
In prison, and here be coffined, when I die.
Here are God's conduits, grave divines; and here
Nature's secretary, the Philosopher.[9]

Nevertheless, he consents to tour the bustling life of the
city with the courtier, who greets 'Every fine, silken, painted
fool we meet' (line 72). On their journey they encounter numerous fools, avoiding grave and sensible figures. Each time the
courtier speaks Donne's speaker replies with a withering insult,
culminating in the final meeting with a 'many-coloured pea-
cock' (92). The courtier admires the fashionable clothes he
wears and then imitates his stoop because he thinks it is part
of a new style imported from France or Italy. As the speaker
warns him, he is right, but only because it is a symptom of the
pox brought back from the courtier's adventures on the Grand
Tour.[10] The young man leaves, spying his love in a window,
'Violently ravished to his lechery' (108). The lady in question
is clearly a woman of easy virtue and the 'motley humorist'
finds that he is no longer in control of the social situation:

Many were there: he could command no more;
He quarrelled, fought, bled, and, turned out of the
    door,
    Directly came to me hanging the head,
    And constantly a while must keep his bed.
    (109–12)

The courtier ends up having to retreat from society in spite
of his wishes, an ironic mirroring of the poet's stated wishes

at the start of the satire. In fact, he avoids having to be away from the buzz of city life for longer by luck rather than judgement, the beating he receives from the men outside his lady's door saving him from a dose of the pox and a lengthy spell of recuperation (or worse).

The courtier may well be an alter ego of the poet himself, suggesting that the city is both a curse (because of its vice) and a cure (because it gives him something to write about). The moralist and the social butterfly are really one and the same creature. Therefore the satire could well be an ironic comment on Donne's representation of himself in his erotic verse, the beating or the pox being seen as a just reward for the sexual exploits narrated elsewhere in poems such as the elegy 'To His Mistress Going to Bed'. Books are vital for the poet, but the satire cannot be written if he is not in the city, hence the need for him to participate in, but also to be distanced from, its life. He needs London as Juvenal needed Rome. Like Juvenal's, Donne's satires make the case that vice has always been a vital part of human nature and cannot simply be dismissed or avoided.

Donne's Satyre 3 describes mankind's ongoing search for true religion and the apparently impossible task of sorting out the wheat from the chaff. The speaker expresses the fear that new developments in religious observance are no more than 'fashions' (line 57), as superficial in their way as the whims of courtly behaviour. Truth, he informs us, is hard to reach, something that is almost impossible to understand, but, like London, it cannot be avoided if one wants to write. Donne's sense of his duty as a poet in the satires may well be Juvenalian in spirit, but his concern with contemporary religious issues also marks the distance that mankind has travelled from classical Rome. In his penultimate satire Juvenal indulges in a rare digression about man's innate foolishness: 'Mankind was on the decline while Homer / Still lived; and today the earth breeds a race of degenerate / Weaklings, who stir high heaven to laughter and loathing' (78–80). Donne is able to qualify Juvenal's pessimism with his religious faith: 'So perish souls which more choose men's unjust / Pow'r from God claimed, than God himself to trust' (Satyre 3, 109–10). The religious context has changed with Christian revelation, but the representation of

Claes Visscher's panorama print of London, 1616.

urban men (and women) in both sets of satires is similar as Donne translates what he can of the literary culture of early imperial Rome to late Elizabethan England.

Donne's reaction to the culture of Petrarchan verse that had come to dominate English poetry in the 1580s and 1590s is more ambivalent.[11] Petrarchan poetry was by no means a monolithic entity; neither did much of it owe anything other than the most superficial of debts to the work of Francesco Petrarca (1304–1374).[12] Petrarch was probably the most influential poet in late medieval and Renaissance Europe through the dissemination of his large and varied collection of Italian lyric poems, *The Canzoniere* (or *Rime Sparse*). These describe the effects of the poet meeting an unobtainable, beautiful woman, Laura, to whom he remained dedicated even though she married another man and then died young. Laura's beauty led Petrarch to a spiritual awareness and an eventual appreciation of the majesty of God's grace. His poetry is characterized by its Christian Neoplatonism, specifically the belief that earthly goods are an inferior copy of the ideal forms that God has established in heaven. Love on earth is to be treasured but it provides only the most fleeting glimpse of the rich rewards that are to be enjoyed in the afterlife for those who are able to enter heaven.[13]

One of Petrarch's most celebrated lyrics, a sonnet, describes how the poet had a wonderful vision of a deer:

A Doe of purest white upon the grass
wearing two horns of gold appeared to me
between two streams beneath a laurel's shade
at sunrise in that season not yet ripe.

The sight of her was so sweetly austere
that I left all my work to follow her,
just like a miser who in search of treasure
with pleasure makes his effort bitterless.

'No one touch me,' around her lovely neck
was written out in diamonds and in topaz,
'It pleased my Caesar to create me free.'

The sun by now had climbed the sky midway,
my eyes were tired but not full from looking
when I fell into water, and she vanished.[14]

The doe is Laura, who is dead and appears before Petrarch
to lead him away from his sinful earthly life to a spiritual one.
The imagery of the octave marks her out as intensely desirable,
the woman as deer being hunted by the man being a common
image in European love poetry (in English, the pun is often
on hart/heart hunting). However, the sestet reveals that she is
unobtainable because she is promised to a higher lord, Caesar,
who stands for God. The poet is still blinded by his earthly
passion, not yet realizing the religious dimension of his love
and needing further guidance from the lady to bring him to
true enlightenment. His fall into water associates him with
the earthly elements below the moon, unready for the ascent
to heaven.

Petrarch's work pervades European poetry of the fifteenth
and sixteenth centuries. Writers adapted his Neoplatonism,
often in rather less strictly religious forms; wrote elaborate
sonnets about remote ladies who had enormous power over

their lives; and made use of his characteristic antitheses, the most frequently imitated example being 'I freeze in fire and burn in ice.' Petrarch was introduced as a significant model for English poets to imitate by Sir Thomas Wyatt and Henry Howard, Earl of Surrey, both poets at the court of Henry VIII. Wyatt adapted Petrarch's *Canzoniere* 190 as the sonnet 'Whoso list to hunt', retaining the central conceit of the lover hopelessly pursuing a deer who informs him that she has been claimed by Caesar, but transforming the poem into a narrative about an earthly lover whom he is prevented from having as his mistress by a more powerful man (undoubtedly the king himself). This poem, along with other poems by Wyatt and Surrey, and other writers, was published in the first printed verse miscellany in English, Richard Tottel's *Songes and Sonettes* (1557). The title clearly had an influence on the title of Donne's love poems when they were published as *Songs and Sonnets* in the first collected edition of his verse in 1633 (though, of course, Donne was dead when they were published and may have had nothing to do with the title).

Donne appears to react against prevailing Petrarchan conventions in his poetry. At times he represents women as equals, at others as despicable creatures (although perhaps no more contemptible than the men he represents in the satires). He rarely represents women as perfect and distant beauties who can ennoble their men, as many poets had done, and he pushes Petrarchan antitheses to absurd limits, notably in the comparison between the lovers and a pair of compasses in 'A Valediction Forbidding Mourning'. Furthermore, he rejects the jog-trot iambic pentameter and conspicuously poetic diction of much Italianate English verse in favour of harsher rhythms and more colloquial speech forms.

However, it would be a mistake to imagine that Donne simply burst onto the poetic scene and transformed everything in one fell swoop. The vogue for Petrarchan poetry was often inherently shrouded in irony. Sir Philip Sidney (1554–1586), whose long sonnet sequence *Astrophil and Stella* had started the vogue for such volumes in Elizabethan England, made use of Petrarch and Petrarchanism in both admiring and sardonic ways. In Sonnet 15 Astrophil argues that poets looking for inspiration should turn away from earlier poetry and simply use the example of Stella. He refers to 'poore *Petrarch's* long deceased woes', as if his work were now dated and old-fashioned, a reference that reminds the reader that Sidney's sequence is anything but ignorant of previous poetry, and that many of the poems are intensely Petrarchan in nature.[15] The reference to Petrarch also alerts the reader to Sidney's grand poetic ambitions – as Donne was to have later – knowing the value of Petrarch's work, but also wishing to advance English poetry beyond it through his own efforts. Sidney, like Donne, indulges in elaborate conceits that push the stock characteristics of Petrarchan poetry as far as they will go. Sonnet 9 opens with the syntactically unusual line 'Queene *Vertue's* court, which some call Stella's face'. Sidney reverses the usual mode of poetic comparison to emphasize the power and majesty that Stella has over him, a common theme in English Petrarchan poetry. The poem is, as the opening suggests, an elaborate description of Stella's face. Her visage is 'Alablaster pure'; her hair is a golden roof; her mouth, a door of 'Red Porphir, which lock of pearl makes sure'; her cheeks are porches made of red and white marble; and her eyes of black touchstone. This magnificent edifice leaves the poet helplessly in her thrall, a sign perhaps of his naivety, and the fact that he is constructing an ideal woman without any relation to the real one he is representing.

Astrophil demonstrates that the Neoplatonic ideal of love is unworkable in a witty, anti-Petrarchan sonnet that takes apart the platitudinous and reductive philosophy practised in Petrarch's name:

> Who will in fairest book of Nature know
> How Vertue may best lodg'd in beautie be,
> Let him but learne of *Love* to reade in thee,
> *Stella*, those faire lines which true goodnesse show.
> There shall he find all vices' overthrow,
> Not by rude force, but sweetest soveraigntie
> Of reason, from whose light those night-birds flie,
> That inward sunne in thine eyes shineth so:
> And not content to be Perfection's heire
> Thy selfe, doest strive all minds that way to move,
> Who marke in thee what is in thee most faire,
> So while thy beautie drawes the heart to love,
> As fast thy Vertue bends that love to good:
> 'But ah,' Desire still cries, 'give me some food.'
> (Sonnet 71)

The last line spectacularly undercuts the previous thirteen, introducing a note of bathos into Astrophil's attempt to persuade the reader that Stella, as Laura did for Petrarch, will lead him to spiritual enlightenment. Astrophil is too base a lover to imitate the Italian master. His journey takes him back down to earth and his god is that of the flesh not the soul. The book of Nature tells him that he cannot escape the tyranny of the flesh, an irony given that he is reading it in the hope of learning the opposite lesson. The poem is also, of course, an acknowledgement that a poetic tradition does not necessarily describe reality, a truth that we are then invited to apply to Sidney's sequence.

Donne's reaction to a Petrarchan tradition was rather more savage than Sidney's, partly, one suspects, because he was writing nearly two decades later, by which time such poets as Sir John Davies had already characterized the Petrarchan lover as 'a patiente burden-bearing Asse' in his manuscript collection 'Gullinge Sonnets', written in the 1590s.[16] Furthermore, as Achsah Guibbory has persuasively argued, many of the more obviously misogynistic poems, which cast women in the power of men, are undoubtedly 'the product of, and a reaction to, the historical situation of England's rule by a woman'.[17] The second edition of Donne's poems in 1635 began with 'The Flea' and 'The Good Morrow', two love poems probably written for his wife, but they were followed and balanced by two assaults on women's characters, 'Song' ('Go, and catch a falling star') and 'Womans Constancy', sending a clear warning to the reader not to expect standard Petrarchan fare. The 'Song', which may be designed to stand as a pointed contrast to the romantic lyrics collected in a volume such as Thomas Campion's *A Book of Airs* (1601), is a light, scornful piece, listing a series of impossible tasks before daring the reader to find a constant woman:

If thou beest born to strange sights,
Things invisible to see,
Ride ten thousand days and nights
Till age snow white hairs on thee:
Thou, when thou return'st, wilt tell me
All strange wonders that befell thee,
   And swear
   'Nowhere
Lives a woman true, and fair.'[18]

The poem bears a striking resemblance to the task that the old woman sets for the rapist knight in Chaucer's *The Wife of Bath's Tale*, which Donne could have read in a number of editions published in the late sixteenth or early seventeenth century.[19] In order to save his life, Chaucer's protagonist has to find out what women want and, after a long quest, discovers that no answers he receives from women asked are the same. Eventually he is told by an aged crone that women want the power to choose, which proves truer than he realizes when she asks to marry him as her reward. Donne's speaker has no idea where his quest will end, his cynical voice suspecting that even the appearance of fidelity will offer no hope of resolution:

Though at the next door we might meet:
Though she were true, when you met her,
And last till you write your letter,
   Yet she
   Will be
False, ere I come, to two, or three. (22–7)

Thomas Hoccleve, 'The Progenie of Geoffrey Chaucer', frontispiece to Thomas Speight, ed., *The Workes of our Ancient and learned English Poet, Geoffrey Chaucer* (1602).

The last line injects a note of humour into the poem, reminding the reader not to take it all too seriously – and, in the process, perhaps challenging any initial sense that this is a lyric written just for the eyes of men. The speaker's assertion that the woman will prove false once he has visited two or three more constructs an image of both sexes playing the field and complaining about each other's lack of constancy. The same representation of sexuality is continued in the next poem in the 1633 volume, 'Womans Constancy', which opens with the striking couplet: 'Now thou hast loved me one whole day, / Tomorrow when thou leav'st, what wilt thou say?'[20] The volume perhaps asks us to read the poem in the light of the fickle and myopic speaker of the previous poem. Certainly, the style and language of both poems is similarly anti-Petrarchan, the narrator in 'Women's Constancy' complaining:

> For having purposed change and falsehood, you
> Can have no way but falsehood to be true?
> Vain lunatic! Against these scapes I could
> > Dispute, and conquer, if I would,
> > > Which I abstain to do,
> For by tomorrow, I may think so too. (12–16)

The poem is frequently dated to the 1590s, which may be right. But it could have been written in a later period, possibly even after the Gunpowder Plot (1605). The plot ended the early period of James's reign when he sought to relax punishment for religious dissidents in the hope of uniting the different strands of religious belief under the single authority of the monarch.[21] After the plot – whether it was a real threat or exaggerated and distorted by James's manipulative ministers – James imposed the Oath of Allegiance, which forced subjects to declare their allegiance to the secular authorities and renounce the legitimacy of any religious power, specifically the Pope.[22] If it was written later than is often assumed, then Donne's poem looks far more like a reflection on the paranoia of the times, in which nobody told the truth because everybody had a motive to lie and be deceitful, than a misogynistic tirade. The last lines suggest that even the most constant of lovers will become duplicitous because they will not be able to keep any oath they swear, however hard they try and whatever they imagine they will do.[23] Put another way, everyone turns lunatic in such times, dominated by the power of the moon to change everything, the only constancy being inconstancy.

Such poems are not simply light, scornful works that expose the ridiculous and out-dated traditions of poetry that had taken hold of literary culture in England in the late sixteenth and early seventeenth century. They are also ways of searching for certainty and security in an uncertain, chaotic world: evidence, perhaps, that Donne was troubled by the difficult political circumstances under which he lived and saw his marriage as a unique example of proper 'Woman's Constancy' when inconstancy dominated. The figures in his poetry, in contrast, are often represented as restless, dissatisfied and superficial characters with no depth or substance, whatever the complexities of the arguments they are capable of spinning. Donne's best poetry is adept at relating the superficial to the profound, connecting the demotic and the philosophical.

John de Critz (attrib.), *James I of England*, c. 1605, oil on canvas.

II

Donne's poetry was informed by other aspects of his wide
and deep reading. His theological and religious reading has
already been discussed but it is also important to note his
interest in diverse strands of philosophy. Again, he is particularly concerned with an understanding of the soul and its
relationship to the body and his willingness to think through
unconventional ideas, as he was in *Biathanatos*. In the long, unfinished poem 'Metempsychosis', written around 1600–1601
(the preface is dated 16 August 1601) while he was working
for Sir Thomas Egerton, Donne explores the implications of
the Pythagorean doctrine that souls could transmute from
one body to another.[24]

In his sermons Donne was more obviously orthodox, dis-
missing unorthodox Christian ideas as heretical fantasies:

> As there is nothing so fantastical and so absurd, but
> that some Hereticks have held it Dogmatically; so
> *Aquinas* notes here, that there were Hereticks that held,
> that the very soul of *Adam* was by a long circuit and
> transmigration come at last into *Paul*, and so *Paul* was
> the same man (in his principal part, in the soul) as *Adam*
> was; and in that sense it was literally true that he said,
> he was *primus peccatorum* the first of all sinners, because
> he was the first man *Adam*: but this is an heretical fancy,
> & a Pythagorean bubble.[25]

'Metempsychosis' is not to be taken entirely seriously –
despite the often intense and serious critical discussions of

the poem – and it is called a 'Poema Satyricon' by its author, after the Menippean satire by Petronius, being a narrative that contains a wide range of styles that imitate, parody and attack a series of targets.[26] The preface makes clear to the reader that this learned poem will challenge a reader and cannot be taken at face value:

> The Pythagorean doctrine doth not only carry one soul from man to man, nor man to beast, but indifferently to plants also; and therefore you must not grudge to find the same soul in an emperor, in a post-horse, and in a mushroom, since no unreadiness in the soul but an indisposition in the organs works this. And there-fore, though this soul could not move when it was a melon, yet it may remember and now tell me at what lascivious banquet it was served. And though it could not speak when it was a spider, yet it can remember and now tell me who used it for poison to attain dignity.[27]

The opening parodies the beginnings of Latin poems, with their invocations to the Muses:

> I sing of the progress of a deathlesse soule,
> Whom Fate, which God made but doth not control,
> Placed in most shapes; all times before the Law
> Yoaked us, and when, and since, in this I sing;
> And th'great world to his aged evening
> From infant morn, through manly noon I draw.
> (1–6)

Donne combines an opening such as that of Virgil's *Aeneid*,
'I sing of arms and of the man, fated to be an exile, who
long since left the land of Troy and came to Italy,' and that
of Ovid's *Metamorphoses*, 'My purpose is to tell of bodies
which have been transformed into shapes of a different kind.
You heavenly powers, since you were responsible for those
changes, as for all else, look favourably on my attempts.'[28]
In Ovid's poem the gods are firmly in control of what happens, which is exactly what Donne denies is taking place
in his, and readers would, of course, have known that God
would not allow pre-Christian souls to go their own way but
would have had their place in a universe after Revelation.
'Metempsychosis' alerts readers to the progress of a soul that
is a fantasy that God would never have permitted to take
place. Indeed, the poem acknowledges this divine control in
its fourth stanza, as the narrator prays to God to ensure that
his story is true: 'Great Destiny, the Commissary of God, /
That hast marked out a path and period / For everything; who,
where wee of-spring tooke, / Our ways and ends, seest at one
instant' (31–4). A central joke in the poem is that mankind
actually degenerates as it gets more sophisticated – a witty,
satirical point, but hardly one that Donne would have truly
believed.[29]

We learn that this very masculine 'great soul' (61), perhaps
the king's powerful minister Robert Cecil (1563–1612), who
was thought to control religious policy in the early seventeenth century, is characterized by the heat and energy that
were supposed to define males in humoral theory. The soul
is too great to be contained in Noah's ark, in which 'The
Church, and all the monarchies did float' (22).[30] It began

life in the apple on the Tree of Knowledge, so has been with mankind from the beginning. It is both innocent and guilty, associated with the taint of original sin without actually being a cause or an effect:

> . . . t'her whom the first man did wive
> (Whom and her race, only forbiddings drive)
> He gave it, she, t'her husband; both did eat;
> So perishèd the eaters, and the meat,
> And we (for treason taints the blood) thence die
>   and sweat. (86–90)

The lines are a mixture of jaunty burlesque, satire and serious religious comment that are, therefore, unsettling in tone and style. There is the familiar misogynistic representation of Eve as the mother of all our ills, but the sophisticated nature of the poem – as elsewhere in Donne – warns us that we should not accept this particular explanation of the Fall. The last line cited here, however, is far more sinister. The reminder that treason taints the blood is surely a reference to the brutal treason laws of the sixteenth century and their use by Elizabeth to suppress Catholic opposition, enabling the state to confiscate the property of traitors.[31] Mary I had executed Protestants for heresy, burning them alive to purify their souls.[32] Elizabeth declared Catholics traitors, something Donne experienced at first hand with his brother, Henry, who would have been found guilty of treason had he not died in prison. For the Protestant state, the Catholic Donne family had a tainted bloodline. Here the line could mean that we are all guilty of original sin as official Christian doctrine,

SERO, SED SERIO

Protestant and Catholic, dictated, or it could imply that some, whatever the truth, are thought to be more guilty than others.

The next three stanzas continue the discussion of original sin. Stanza 10 confirms the suspicion that the sexist comments blaming Eve for the Fall are ironic. That verse concludes,

John de Critz (attrib.), *Robert Cecil, 1st Earl of Salisbury*, 1602, oil on panel.

'Shee sinned, we bear; part of our pain is, thus / To love them whose fault to this painful love yoked us' (99–100). The newly married Donne was clearly reflecting that he could not survive without women and that, even if their sins damned mankind, he had no intention of living alone. The following stanzas debate the nature of the Fall and what we might be able to do about the knowledge we have of it, more lines that are both serious and ironic:

> So fast in us doth this corruption grow,
> That now wee dare aske why wee should be so.
> Would God (disputes the curious rebel) make
> A law, and would not have it kept? Or can
> His creatures will, cross his? Of every man
> For one, will God (and be just) vengeance take?
> Who sinn'd? T'was not forbidden to the snake
> Nor her, who was not then made; nor is't writ
> That Adam cropped or knew the apple; yet
> The worm and she, and he, and wee endure for it.
>
> But snatch me Heav'nly Spirit from this vain
> Reckoning their vanities; less is their gain
> Then hazard still to meditate on ill,
> Though with good mind; their reason's, like those
>   toys
> Of glassy bubbles, which the gamesome boys
> Stretch to so nice a thinness through a quill
> That they themselves break, do themselves spill,
> Arguing is heretics' game, and exercise,
> As wrestlers, perfects them; Not liberties

Of speech, but silence, hands, not tongues, end
    heresies. (101–20)

The lines resemble standard theological debates about the
nature and origin of sin, articulated elsewhere by Donne in
poems such as 'To Christ', in which the speaker wonders how
God could ever forgive him for his countless sins, and, of
course, in many of Donne's sermons.[33] Here, however, the
questions asked are so fundamental as to seem either naive or
sceptical. Would God make laws that no one could keep and
then seek to punish everyone as a perpetrator? Will he be
revenged on everyone – that is, will everyone go to hell whatever the nature of their sins and the state of their souls? These
might seem like sensible questions until we hear the speaker
state that it was not forbidden for the snake to sin. Now, the
reader with even the most basic Christian theology understands that the speaker has no concept of Christ's sacrifice and
the resulting *felix culpa* (happy fall). The words are spoken by
someone who is profoundly ignorant; someone who, the poem
implies, takes Pythagoras' notion of metempsychosis seriously,
believing all souls – vegetable, animal and mineral – to be equal.
    The following stanza is equally ironic, the speaker suggest-
ing that, as a result of the complex nature of understanding
the soul and our purpose in the universe, we should, therefore,
simply ask no questions about anything. This was, in essence,
fideism (although that term was not coined until near the
end of the nineteenth century), a position often attributed
to Michel de Montaigne (1533–1592), whose ideas may have
influenced Donne's poem.[34] It was not Donne's position and
he explored and debated theological questions throughout

his life, often pursuing unorthodox, even heretical, arguments in order to clarify his thinking, with 'Metempsychosis' being an obvious example. Arguing may well be a 'heretics' game, and exercise', but it is one that Donne was prepared to risk. The final line is another reminder that there were worse things than argument: 'hands, not tongues, end heresies' suggests that they also end the lives of those accused of heresy – again, a reminder of the terrible fate of his mother's most famous ancestor, Thomas More, as well as his brother Henry.

The rest of the poem charts the progress of the soul as it passes from body to body, plant to plant and creature to creature. Starting as a plant in the Garden of Eden, the soul inhabits a sparrow and soon after passes into a fish, which is devoured by a swan. Cast out from the swan (Donne makes a number of coy references to excretion), the soul ends up inside another fish, which leads the speaker to reflect on imprisonment:

> Now swam a prison in a prison put,
> And now this soul in double walls was shut
> Till, melted with the Swans digestive fire,
> She left her house the fish, and vapoured forth;
> Fate, not affording bodies of more worth
> For her as yet, bids her again retire
> T'another fish, to any new desire
> Made a new prey; for he that can to none
> Resistance make, nor complaint, sure is gone.
> Weakness invites, but silence feasts oppression.
> (241–50)

On the one hand these lines are a fairly common image associated with Neoplatonic belief, of the soul imprisoned within the body waiting for release so that it can soar up to heaven, frequently employed by Donne.[35] On the other they refer, again, to the experience of Catholics and others who had suffered for their belief under the Elizabethan regime.[36] The final lines are both satirical and poignant: crushed into silence, how could most Catholics under Elizabeth's rule – rather than those in exile – be expected to foster serious opposition to the regime? Moreover, should they want to? Donne can hardly have expected a straightforward answer, or given one himself. He had been silent and it is not clear whether he was still a Catholic at all, his writing more often than not opposing those who tried to police an individual's belief.[37] Only a few years later he would write *Pseudo-Martyr*, which attempted to outline the ways in which a nation beset by religious division could function and thrive.

The soul remains as a fish for the next few stanzas, eventually having to escape from a whale killed by a number of smaller, aggressive fish, specifically the swordfish and the shark. The whale's death leads the speaker to consider the significance of the death of monarchs, lines that seem to reflect on the nature of regime change, which was a pressing subject in 1601:

Who will revenge his death? Or who will call
Those to account that thought, and wrought his fall?
Th'heirs of slain kings, we see, are often so
Transported with the joy of what they get,
That they revenge and obsequies forget;

Nor will against such men the people go,
Because he's now dead, to whom they should show
Love in that act. Some kings by vice being grown
So needy of subjects' love, that of their own
They think they lose, if love be to the dead Prince
    shown. (361–70)

Again, Donne's lines are careful and studied in their ambiguity. Ostensibly they read as a warning to monarchs not to
ignore or forget the recently deceased ruler whom they have
replaced, in particular if they have obtained the throne via
an assassination. But they also analyse the nature of government, wondering how much monarchs should listen to
their subjects – too much attention to their desires may be
an error if it prevents rulers from doing the right thing and
governing well, especially if the love for a former monarch
causes backward-looking policies. The stanza can equally be
read as a warning of the immediate dangers and conflicted
loyalties that dynastic change, however planned and peaceful,
will bring. Moreover, in the Protestant imagination violent
political acts (assassinations, coups d'état) were the policies
of militant Catholics – specifically, Jesuits – and would inevitably cause the most serious problems. While Donne appears
eager to see debate about religion, against the wishes of most
rulers, he is equally clear that political debate, especially if it
leads to direct action, is best avoided.

The soul next seeks refuge in a mouse, choosing a small
body after inhabiting such a large one. Unfortunately this ends
badly too. The mouse crawls up an elephant's trunk and gnaws
the poor beast's brain until it collapses and dies. It next passes

into a wolf cub, then an ape, entertaining Adam and Eve and
their family, before the creature is stoned to death by Tethemite,
one of Adam's sons. Now it assumes human form:

> . . . keeping some quality
> Of every past shape, she knew treachery,
> Rapine, deceit, and lust, and ills enow
> To be a woman. Themech she is now,
> Sister and wife to Cain, Cain that first did plough.
> (506–10)

We are back to the misogynistic sentiments expressed at the
start of the poem, perhaps a sign that metempsychosis leads
nowhere and simply repeats itself as a belief and as a process,
as the soul flits from host to host, having a wealth of experiences without ever really developing. The progress of a
human soul should be one of growth and enlightenment, as
Donne charted in his more serious poems on the subject, *The
Anniversaries*, written a decade later.[38]

It is hard to judge the significance of 'Metempsychosis',
as it appears to be either unfinished or hastily finished, surviv-
ing only in manuscript until it was published in 1633; unless
the return to a frivolous misogyny has a particular significance
in rounding the poem off.[39] The poem satirizes superficial
thought about religion alongside a series of barbed comments
warning rulers that the consequences of persecution will be
widespread fear and a failure to engage seriously with complicated theological ideas and problems, impeding the progress
of the soul. Instead of moving forward towards God, people
will just turn round in circles like the souls moving from body

to body in the poem. 'Metempsychosis' is an important Donne poem, a mixture of the profound and the superficial, the humorous and the serious, the author's learning deployed in an unsettling, possibly even dangerous, manner, to discomfort and challenge the reader. Rather like so many of his lyrics.

SIX

Friendship

hile Donne had a significant reputation as a poet and a preacher, he was also known as a friend. As he stated in one of his most frequently quoted lines, written when he thought he was dying in late 1623:

> No Man is an Iland, intire of it selfe; every man is a peece of the Continent . . . Any Mans death diminishes me, because I am involved in Mankinde; And therefore never send to know for whom the *bell* tolls; It tolls for *thee*.[1]

Donne placed great value on his connections to other people. They were companions on earth, helping to make life more bearable and, if all went well, would remain so in the afterlife. Death would either lead to the greater union of friends – and anyone *could* be a friend – or the sadness of eternal separation.

The publication of *Letters to Several Persons of Honour* by Donne's son in 1651, when read alongside the large number of verse letters that had appeared in the same editor's volume of his father's poems (1633), showed that Donne had dedicated a great deal of time and effort to cultivating relationships

with his peers, both men and women. Indeed a large number of Donne's manuscripts are verse letters, a significant fact given his preference for circulating much of his work in that form to close friends.[2] Of course, some of the letters published were addressed to patrons, but the majority were written to

P. Lombart, 'John Donne', frontispiece to John Donne, *Poems, by J. D. With Elegies on the Authors Death* (1633).

POEMS,

By J. D.

WITH

ELEGIES

ON THE AUTHORS

DEATH.

LONDON.
Printed by *M. F.* for I O H N M A R R I O T,
and are to be fold at his fhop in St *Dunftans*
Church-yard in *Fleet-ftreet.* 1 6 3 3.

people whom Donne held dear and wished to communicate
with as equals: Bridget White (later Lady Kingsmill), to
whom Donne wrote five somewhat flirtatious letters that
open the volume; Sir Thomas Lucy, addressed as 'Your very
true and earnest friend and servant and lover', one of Donne's

Title page to John Donne, *Poems, by J. D. With Elegies on the Authors Death*
(1633).

familiar and intimate modes of address; Sir Henry Goodere, a close friend, scribe and frequent correspondent who receives by far the largest number of letters in the volume;[3] Sir Henry Wotton, another old friend from Donne's time at Oxford, well known as a correspondent and friend of many significant writers, intellectuals and powerful people;[4] Sir Edward Herbert, Lord of Cherbury, who was sent a copy of *Biathanatos*, as was Sir Robert Carr; Donne's patron, Lucy Harington, Countess of Bedford; and others. Many, along with other friends and patrons, had already been linked to Donne through the verse letters published in the volume of poems.

Friendship was a central ideal in Renaissance culture and the adage, made famous by Erasmus, 'Friends hold all things in common' was a basic principle that many held dear.[5] The Renaissance ideal of friendship was that of a relationship between equals where free and unrestrained conversation could take place and the pressures of the outside world, with its insistence of hierarchies and the need for deferential respect of social superiors, could be suspended. Ben Jonson, another friend in Donne's circle, provides a clear sense of what friendship involved in his poem 'On Inviting a Friend to Supper' (published 1616):

> Tonight, grave sir, both my poor house and I
> > Do equally desire your company;
> Not that we think us worthy such a guest,
> > But that your worth will dignify our feast,
> With those that come, whose grace may make that seem
> > Something, which else could hope for no esteem.[6]

Jonson is following one of his favourite authors – Martial – and, as in Martial's poem of invitation, Jonson then lists the food they will be able to share even as he laments the limitations of his table: olives, capers and salad, then mutton and hen in lemon and wine sauce, as well as a variety of game birds.[7] The joke, one Jonson makes elsewhere, is at his own expense: a comment on his gargantuan appetites and corpulent body.[8] But it is also a celebration of the pleasures of equality and unrestrained discussion between equals. During

Abraham van Blyenberch, *Ben Jonson*, c. 1617, oil on canvas.

the meal Jonson's servant will 'read a piece of Virgil, Tacitus, / Livy, or of some better book to us' (21–2), and the guests will be able to discuss what they hear without fear: 'we'll speak our minds amidst our meat' (23). The poem concludes with words that make it clear that the meal is as much about the need to exercise the political ideal of friendship as it is a celebration of eating and drinking:

> And we shall have no Poley or Parrot by,
> Nor shall our cups make any guilty men:
>   But, at our parting, we will be as when
> We innocently met. No simple word
>   That shall be uttered at our mirthful board
> Shall make us sad next morning, or affright
>   The liberty that we'll enjoy tonight. (36–42)

These last lines are a sharp reminder that the world outside the trust engendered in proper friendship circles could be dangerous and cruel. Robert Poley and William Parrot were notorious informers, Poley having helped ensnare and kill Jonson's fellow playwright Christopher Marlowe – significantly enough, after supper.[9] Jonson might well have suffered at their hands after one of his frequent clashes with the law.[10] In contrast, within the closed circle of their table talk, the host and guests can say exactly what they want, knowing that no careless statements will have any consequences the next day. They will remain innocent and able to enjoy the liberty that friendship affords people who take the virtue seriously, whatever they discuss. Drink will be used as a stimulus to friendly conversation and not as a means of distorting words in order to incriminate and ensnare those whose opinions may be at odds with official doctrine.

Donne's language in many of his letters tries to establish the equality required between friends, although, when addressing patrons, it is clear that he mingles solicitude and deference with sympathy and empathy. The letters to Sir Henry Goodere perhaps give the best sense of Donne at his most chatty and intimate, as he ranges widely over a number of subjects that the two men obviously discuss together in private, sharing their thoughts via manuscript:

> Sir,
> Every Tuesday I make account that I turn a great hour-glass, and consider that a weeks life is run out since I writ. But if I aske my self what I have done in the last watch, or would do in the next, I can say nothing; if I say that I have passed it without hurting any, so may the Spider in my window. The primitive Monkes were excusable in their retirings and enclosures of themselves: for even of them every one cultivated his own garden and orchard, that is, his soul and body, by meditation, and manufactures; and they ought the world no more since they confirmed none of her sweetnesse, nor begot others to burden her. But for me, if I were able to husband all my time so thriftily, as not onely not to wound my soul in any minute by actuall sinne, but not to rob and cousin her by giving any part to pleasure or businesse, but bestow it all upon her in meditation, yet even in that I should wound her more, and contract another guiltinesse.[11]

The letter begins almost dramatically, *in medias res*, as if the two men are carrying on a conversation, clearly attempting to recapture the immediacy of face-to-face contact. Donne's carefully constructed sentences juxtapose and mix together different subjects and registers, moving easily between the jocular and the serious (as he does in many poems). On the one hand he is simply telling his friend that he is not getting on with very much and is wasting a lot of time; on the other he is exploring the vital question of how we should live life and how we might make the best use of our time, as we have so little of it and are aware that it rapidly slides away. Details of what he can see in his house (the spider in the window) are placed next to reflections on how ancient monks lived, a recollection from his theological reading, which also serves as a post-Reformation comment, because monks had, of course, disappeared in England after the break with Rome. The final sentence cited here is also a mixture of the trivial and the profound. Donne worries about wasting his time, which may lead him into sinful thoughts if not actions (another familiar theological conundrum), but again, the addressee would realize that this comment is also a means of passing the time, establishing friendship through writing, but not actually achieving anything substantial. Donne would appear to be wondering aloud whether he should be writing a serious work — such as *Pseudo-Martyr* or a sermon — or writing to a friend. The letter may even have been written with possible publication in mind, as there were significant volumes of ancient and modern letters published, many designed to represent the virtues of friendship, although this is unlikely given Donne's reticence about appearing in print and his clear preference for controlling his work through manuscript circulation.[12]

Goodere (bap. 1571–1627) was one of Donne's closest friends, probably from the late 1580s onwards, both having a Catholic background and a number of common interests and mutual friends. He was part of the large circle of young men who gravitated towards Robert Devereux, 2nd Earl of Essex, the rising star of the 1590s, and one of Essex's many followers who were knighted during his disastrous Irish campaign of 1599.[13] He had a relatively successful court career under James, becoming a Gentleman of the Privy Chamber (like another of Donne's friends, Sir Robert Drury), and he took part in various masques, including Jonson's *Hymenaei* (1606), but later ran into trouble through some rather intemperate actions.[14] He was cultured and literary, exchanging verse and books with Donne, and he often acted as the carrier of Donne's letters to the Countess of Bedford, which were sent to him with their correspondence.[15] Goodere was recognized as a sociable, clubbable man with a great capacity for friendship, qualities recognized in Jonson's epigrams addressed to him – poems that praise their subject in rather double-edged terms:

> Goodere, I'm glad and grateful to report
>   Myself a witness of thy few days' sport:
> Where I both learned why wise men hawking follow,
>   And why that bird was sacred to Apollo.
> She doth instruct men by her gallant flight
>   That they to knowledge so should tower upright,
> That they never stoop but to strike ignorance;
>   Which if they miss, they yet should re-advance

To former height, and there in circle tarry
  Till they be sure to make the fool their quarry.
Now, in whose pleasures I have this discerned,
  What would his serious actions me have
    learned?[16]

As in so many of Jonson's subtle epigrams, what looks like
praise is actually a warning about poor behaviour and a
reminder that there are rigorous ethical standards that must
be applied in private and public life. Jonson thanks Goodere
for teaching him about hawking, letting the reader know that
he has not practised the sport until well into middle age. The
judgement that hawking instructs its practitioners is also carefully nuanced. Jonson turns the topic to knowledge and the
need to combat ignorance for a position of serious erudition,
clearly reminding Goodere that he spends too much time pursuing an enjoyable sport and so is unable to read its significance,
therefore failing to turn to his books for proper instruction.
In doing so Goodere has become a fool, a quarry (the meat
used to train hawks), who is wasting his talents enjoying the
sport with others, rather than reading, learning and being the
master in charge of his own life. The final couplet ostensibly
means that Goodere is such a skilled sportsman that when he
works on something serious he must be exceptional. But, of
course, this apparent praise is really a demand that he stop
wasting his time and do something productive with his life.[17]

Donne addressed Goodere in one verse letter (although
there may be others that have not survived), written between
1607 and 1609. The poem alludes to the same issues that
occur in Jonson's poem, suggesting that Goodere's problems

were of long standing. Donne advises his friend that he needs
to look after himself better than he has done:

> Provide you manlier diet; you have seen
> > All libraries, which are schools, camps, and courts;
> But ask your garners if you have not been
> > In harvests too indulgent to your sports.[18]

As in Jonson's epigram, Donne reminds his friend that he
is a learned man and that he needs to return to his books in
order to get his life back in order. He also needs to eat more
sensibly, consuming foods that stiffen his manly resolve rather
than indulging in effeminate luxury, and, as Jonson warned
too, curtail his excessive love of hawking.

Donne addresses Goodere more directly than Jonson does,
the verse letter reproducing the style of a conversation with
his friend rather than, as in Jonson's poem, an archly constructed warning to be decoded by both the addressee and the
reader. Donne's advice appears as part of a more general series
of reflections on ageing and wasting time, sentiments that can
be read in terms of his letter to Goodere in which he laments
his own ability to indulge in long unproductive periods:

> Who makes the past a pattern for next year,
> > Turns no new leaf, but still the same things reads:
> Seen things, he sees again, heard things doth hear,
> > And makes his life but like a pair of beads.
>
> A palace, when 'tis that, which it should be,
> > Leaves growing, and stands such, or else decays:

But he, which dwells there is not so, for he
> Strives to urge upward, and his fortune raise;

So had your body her morning, hath her noon,
> And shall not better; her next change is night:
But her fair larger guest, t'whom sun and moon
> Are sparks and short-lived, claims another right.

The noble soul by age grows lustier,
> Her appetite and her digestion mend:
We must not starve, nor hope to pamper her
> With women's milk, and pap unto the end.
> (1–16)

Donne warns his friend that he cannot live in the past, that there are acute dangers in repeating years when we should be moving on as we are getting older and have to change. The image at the end of the first stanza, that the risk of stasis reduces life to 'a pair of beads', is a reference to the rosary, one of the elements of the Catholic faith particularly despised by Protestants as a form of idolatry, concentrating on the image rather than the substance of the faith. One Protestant preacher referred to the instructions provided for rosary use as a 'Sodomiticall, brutish, and Heathenish booke', which would inspire the Lord's vengeance.[19] Donne is surely alluding to the fact that he has moved on from his Catholic faith and embraced a new order, and is urging Goodere to follow his example (perhaps in religion, perhaps in other ways). The body and soul need to move forward and accept that they are ageing, moving closer to the time when they will be reunited with God. Therefore, there is no time to waste because *tempus fugit* (time flies). Donne is consciously speaking to an equal, a friend who shares his own understanding of the world, not saying anything that he would not say to himself (as he does in the letter to Goodere). In contrast, Jonson addressed Goodere as someone who needed the benevolent and wise advice of the poet, his moral guardian.

Donne advises his friend to get out of the rut he is in and to redeem himself through travel, escaping from the pleasures that trap him in his unhealthy physical and spiritual state and prevent him from moving on and growing. He returns to the image of the hawk, speaking a friendly language that he knows Goodere will understand (but which is also an indication of how limited he has become through his neglect of knowledge):

> It pays you well, if it teach you to spare
>   And make you ashamed; to make your hawk's
>   praise yours,
> Which, when herself she lessens in the air,
>   You then first say that high enough she towers.
>   (33–6)

Goodere has let his reputation, his credit, fall to a low level so that he is not taken as seriously as he should be. A person's credit was vital at a time when it was the most significant asset they had, and how they operated in society would depend primarily on how others understood their worth.[20] Goodere needs to stop thinking solely in terms of the hawks he treasures so much and use his favourite sport to realize how he should be seen and valued. Just as the hawk towers over those on the ground, so should Goodere be inspired to have others look up to him. Donne urges Goodere to return to godly ways – implying that he has strayed from them – but concludes the poem, as he began it, linking the two men as friends rather than standing in judgement over him (as Jonson does):

> But thus I make you keep your promise sir:
>   Riding, I had you, though you still stayed there,
> And in these thoughts, although you never stir,
>   You came with me to Mitcham, and ere here.
>   (45–8)

The stanza brings us back to the practicalities of friendship between two men who live some distance apart. Donne has written the poem while riding and is therefore in Goodere's company even though he is not physically present, and, in doing so, he has transported him to his house at Mitcham. The urge to have his friend move is transformed into a plea to have him pay a visit, the humour simultaneously reinforcing and undercutting the serious nature of the poem's message. Goodere may well be in social, spiritual and physical peril, but Donne's parting gesture ensures that he will understand that everyone may well be in the same situation and need to reform and move on.

Sir Henry Wotton was, according to Isaak Walton, a close friend from his Oxford days. Walton wrote lives of both men and claimed that they had an especially deep and lasting friendship, one that resembled a marriage:

The friendship of these two [was] . . . such a friendship as was generously elemented: And as it was began
in their Youth, and in an University, and there main-
tained by correspondent Inclinations and Studies, so
it lasted till Age and Death forced a Separation.[21]

Wotton was among the most successful and high profile
of Donne's friends. Widely travelled in Europe, he entered
the service of the Earl of Essex in the mid-1590s, and served

Unknown artist, *Sir Henry Wotton, c.* 1630–50, oil on canvas.

as his secretary in Ireland, where he was knighted. He was
not implicated in the events leading to Essex's downfall and
execution – unlike another secretary, Henry Cuffe (1562/3–
1601), who was executed along with his master – and became
ambassador to Venice in 1603 after James VI of Scotland
became King James I of England and Ireland. He later served
as ambassador to Savoy, The Hague, and twice again at Venice
before becoming headmaster of Eton. Wotton was well known
as a man of letters, composing a number of poems and coin-
ing the aphorism that an ambassador is an 'honest man sent
to lie abroad for the good of his country' ('Legatus est vir
bonus peregre missus ad mentiendum rei publicae causa').[22]

A number of letters survive that, although not signed and
dated, are almost certainly from Wotton to Donne, as well
as from Donne to Wotton.[23] Donne's letters to Wotton are
informal, witty and talkative, and it is clear that they enjoyed
an extensive correspondence over a long period of time and
that this interaction was important to both of them. In
Ireland in 1599 Wotton answered Donne's complaint that he
had not written often enough:

> It is worth wondering that you can complain of my
> seldom writing, when your own letters come so fear-
> fully, as if they tread all the way upon a bog. I have
> received from you a few, and almost every one hath a
> commission to speak of divers of their fellows, like you
> know whom in the old comedy that asks for the rest
> of his servants. But you make no mention of any of
> mine, yet it is not long since I ventured much of my
> experience unto you in a piece of paper, and perhaps

not of my credit; it is that which I sent you by A. R. [Sir
Alexander Radcliffe?], whereof, till you advertise me,
I shall live in fits or agues.[24]

Wotton's tone is a mixture of irritation, disappointment and
friendly banter. There are shared jokes (the letters coming
slowly because they are treading warily through bogs; Wotton
suffering from fits and agues unless he hears from Donne)
and literary allusions (the stock character in old [ancient
Greek] comedy asking for his servants).

The truth may well have been that it was Donne who had
not written often enough. Another letter seems to acknowledge that this was the case, written after Wotton had returned
suddenly with Essex in September 1599 in a desperate
attempt to persuade the queen that the truce he had signed
with the Earl of Tyrone was part of a serious strategy likely
to bring peace to Ireland:

> This letter hath a greater burthen and charge, for it car-
> ries not only an assurance of myself to you but it begs a
> pardon that I have not in these weeks sought you out
> in England by letters and acknowledged how deep root
> the kindness of your letter hath taken in me.[25]

More likely it was a shared joke between them expressing
their mutual admiration and dependence on each other's
conversation.

Donne enshrined their relationship in a verse letter sent
to Wotton while he was on campaign with Essex in Ireland:

Went you to conquer? And have so much lost
Yourself, that what in you was best and most
Respective friendship should so quickly die?
In public gain my share's not such that I
Would lose that love for Ireland: better cheap
I pardon Death (who though he do not reap
Yet gleans he many of our friends away)
Than that your waking mind should be a prey
To lethargies. Let shots and bogs and skenes
With bodies deal as Fate bids or restrains:
Ere sicknesses attach, young death is best:
Who pays before death doth scape arrest.
Let not the soul, at first with graces filled,
And since, and thorough crooked limbecks stilled
      [stills distilled]
In many schools and courts, which quicken it,
Itself unto the Irish negligence submit.
I ask not laboured letters which should wear
Long papers out, nor letters which should fear
Dishonest carriage, or a seer's art,
Nor such as from the brain comes, but the heart.[26]

The poem centres on the familiar jibe that when transplanted
to Ireland Englishmen and women would be unable to resist
the forces that would make them Irish: indeed, they may
become 'Hiberniores Hibernicis ipsis' ('more Irish than the
Irish themselves').[27] Wotton, in Donne's poem, has become
Irish and forgotten himself and his friend, allowing their
friendship to perish. Donne reminds Wotton that the danger
of death is exceptionally high, especially in Ireland, known

for the high mortality rate of English armies there.[28] The unstated fear here is that Wotton will die there so he needs to hear that he is well and get at least one more letter from him. Donne adapts another familiar cliché, that it is best to die young in order to stave off the pains and humiliations of old age, before turning to his favourite subject, the soul. Donne insists that Wotton must preserve his soul, whatever he experiences in Ireland, keeping his identity as it has always been: that way, even if he does not survive in Ireland, the men's souls will be able to communicate after death. In order to demonstrate that this has not happened, Donne begs a letter from Wotton, one that need not be long, convoluted or learned, but which comes from the heart.

In many ways, and despite its derogatory perception of Ireland and the Irish, the verse letter is a touching poem expressing sincere friendship as a bulwark against the uncertainties and hostilities of the world around them: very similar to the ways in which Donne represents his marriage. Death may separate them, but it is the other forces – in particular, the state of lethargy that Ireland induces in its inhabitants – that is the most pernicious danger the friends have to face.

In a slightly earlier verse letter (*c.* August 1598), Donne had laid out his understanding of letters in characteristically hyperbolic terms:

> Sir, more than kisses, letters mingle souls,
> For, thus friends absent speak. This ease controls
> The tediousness of my life: but for these
> I could ideate [imagine] nothing which could please,
> But I should wither in one day, and pass

> To'a bottle [bundle]' of hay, that am a lock [tuft] of
> grass.[29]

The last line surely refers to the familiar verses in Isaiah
(40:5–8) expressing God's omnipotence:

> And the glory of the LORD shall be revealed, and all
> the flesh shall see *it* together: for the mouth of the
> LORD hath spoken *it*.
> The voice said, Cry. And he said, What shall I cry?
> All flesh is grass, and all the goodliness thereof *is* as
> the flower of the field:
> The grass withereth, the flower fadeth: because
> the spirit of the LORD bloweth upon it: surely the
> people *is* grass.
> The grass withereth, the flower fadeth: but the word
> of our God shall stand for ever.

Donne has transposed the image of flesh as grass to lines
about the soul and immortality. In Isaiah, God's power
stands as a reminder of the fragility of all flesh, which may
be beautiful but is not eternal and so fades and withers as
all plants do. In Donne's verse letter, the letter itself has a
permanence because, despite its ephemeral form, it enables
souls to communicate and so grow together, contributing to
and sustaining their identity. Donne understands that letters
from friends such as Wotton provide him with the medicine
('ease') to combat the boredom of his routine life. Just as he
felt that without the exchange of letters in Ireland Wotton
was in danger of descending into a dangerous lethargy, so

does Donne imagine himself withering without proper com-
munication with his true friends.

Donne and Wotton frequently discussed literary subjects.
In a letter from around 1600 Donne claims, with mock modesty, that he is 'no great voyager in other men's works' before
launching into one of the few discussions of Dante by an
English commentator in the early seventeenth century. His
comments show how literary and theological judgements
could not easily be separated and that readers would take
what profit and instruction they could from the works they
read, as historians of reading have pointed out:

I flung away Dante the Italian, a man pert [clever]
enough, to be beloved and too much to be believed. It
angered me that Celestine, a Pope so far from the man-
ners of other popes that he left even their seat, should
by the court of Dante's wit be attached [arrested] and
by him thrown into his purgatory, and it angered me
as much that in the life of a pope he should spy no
greater fault than that, in the affectation [desire] of a
cowardly security, he slipped from the great burthen
laid upon him. Alas, what would Dante have him do?
Thus we find the story related: he that thought himself
next in succession by a trunk through a wall whispered
in Celestine's ear counsel to remove the papacy. Why
should not Dante be content to think that Celestine
took this for as immediate a salutation and discourse
of the Holy Ghost as Abraham did the commandment
of killing his son? If he will needs punish retiredness
thus, what hell can his wit devise for ambition?[30]

Celestine V was pope for five months in 1294, after the Holy See had been vacant for over two years due to a series of internal divisions and factional in-fighting among the cardinals. Pietro da Morrone was an aged and devout hermit, whose election as Pope Celestine V was initially welcomed before it became obvious that he was merely the puppet of Charles II, king of Sicily and Naples (c. 1254–1309; r. 1285–1309), who used the Pope to put his supporters in powerful ecclesiastical positions. Unhappy in his powerful role, Celestine was assured that there were precedents enabling him to abdicate without damaging the Church – even though there were not – and he stepped down hoping to return to his retreat, but was imprisoned until his death, as his successor Boniface VIII (1294–1303) was worried about conflict and schism.[31]

Dante placed Celestine in the upper regions of Hell (not Purgatory as Donne writes), near the gates, damned because of his feeble betrayal of the Church:

> *Poscia ch'io v'ebbe alcuno riconosciuto,*
> *vidi e conobbi l'ombra di colui*
> *che fece per viltade il gran rifuto.*

> A few I recognised. And then I saw –
> and knew beyond all doubt – the shadow of the one
> who made, from cowardice, the great denial.[32]

Celestine had failed to protect and nurture the Church, the duty of all of its servants, in whatever role they are called to play, putting his own happiness and needs above those of

God and his fellow men and women. By no means as worthy of punishment as the traitors, including Brutus and Cassius, who suffer in the lowest depths of Hell (Canto 34, lines 64–9), Celestine is, nonetheless, one of God's enemies.

Donne's objection to Dante's judgement in the letter to Wotton reveals a great deal. The letter demonstrates that in private friends, as Jonson's poem 'Inviting a Friend to Supper' indicates, were able to discuss difficult, controversial subjects that they would avoid in public life for fear of punishment.

Niccolò di Tommaso, *Pope St Celestine V, c.* 1365–76, detail of centre panel, fresco from the castle at Casaluce, Caserta.

Letters became one of the places where free expression would flourish. Donne's comments suggest that friends could debate complicated issues of the Catholic faith at times when they were best avoided. More specifically, it seems that he was thinking of Celestine's sad fate in terms of his own experience of repressive religious regimes, and his brother's sad death in prison. Donne objects to what he obviously saw as Dante's censorious, judgemental verdict, unfairly condemning someone who was put in an impossible position, rather like so many English Catholics.[33]

If someone whispered in Celestine's ear that it was perfectly acceptable to abdicate, how can he be blamed for what he did, Donne asks. Does not the Bible provide a host of uncomfortable examples of God making what appear to be terrible demands on his loyal servants, like asking a father to sacrifice a son as God asked Abraham (Genesis 22)? Here Donne would appear to be alluding to the fear of being left alone in the world with no spiritual guidance, a common problem for many Christians after the Reformation.[34] Who is able to distinguish without fail between true and false voices? The Pope was supposed to provide the Church with spiritual guidance – a daunting task; and if even the Pope could have such fears and make such mistakes, what hope could there be for anyone else? Demanding punishment for those who seek to retreat from the world is to establish a form of Christianity that asks too much of believers and is far too aggressive and hostile to those who fail to conform. We can see that Donne is already on the road to *Pseudo-Martyr* and suspicious of powerful state Churches that demand conformity from the populations they oversee.

Donne also corresponded with a number of women: some friends, some patrons, sometimes women who were a mixture of the two.[35] The published collection of his correspondence, *Letters to Several Persons of Honour*, opened with two rather coy letters to Mrs Bridget White, perhaps foregrounding Donne's relationship with women to enhance the appeal of the volume to a wide range of readers. Bridget White (d. 1672) was from Hampshire but had evidently encountered Donne when she was staying in London in spring 1610.[36] That summer she married Sir Henry Kingsmill (*c.* 1588–1624) and became a formidable presence within a powerful family; their granddaughter Anne Finch, Countess of Winchilsea (1661–1720), was a successful poet.[37] Donne sent Bridget a number of letters, many of which evidently went astray, and, as in his correspondence with Wotton, he was most insistent that he received the replies he craved. The opening letter (undated) in the collection is an elaborate conceit praising his correspondent in a rather overbearing manner:

> Madame,
> I could make some guesse whether souls that go to heaven, retain any memory of us that stay behind, if I knew whether you ever thought of us, since you enjoyed your heaven, which is your self, at home. Your going away hath made *London* a dead carkasse. A Tearm, and a Court do a little spice and embalme it, and keep it from putrefaction, but the soul went away with you: and I think the onely reason why the plague is somewhat slackned, is, because the place is dead already, and no body left worth the killing. Whereforever you are,

there is *London* enough: and it is a diminishing of you
to say so, since you are more than the rest of the world.
When you have a desire to work a miracle, you will
return hither, and raise the place from the dead, and
the dead that are in it; of which I am one, but that a

William Larkin, *Bridget White, Lady Kingsmill*, before 1619, oil on panel.

hope that I have a room in your favour keeps me alive,
which you shall abundantly confirm to me, if by one
letter you tell me, that you have received my six; for now
my letters are grown to that bulk, that I may divide
them like *Amadis* the *Gaules* book, and tell you, that this
is the first letter of the second part of the first book.
Your humblest, and affectionate
Servant J. D.[38]

The familiar intimate style has a number of resemblances
to that used in the letters to his male friends – in particular,
the drawn-out conceit that employs serious, intellectual vocabulary on matters close to Donne's heart in a frivolous manner,
as a means of establishing a shared joke. On the one hand the
letter suggests that Donne addressed female friends in the
same way that he addressed male friends, especially when we
consider how desperate he was to hear from Sir Henry
Wotton. On the other, however, it could be read as a coercive
act, forcefully reminding a young woman that she had already
received six unanswered letters from him: behaviour that
would now, if not then, be considered extremely questionable.
The letter is certainly flirtatious, with a possibly bawdy quip
about raising the dead (as well as an obvious appeal for patronage, making Donne's supplication a mutually understood
joke), and one wonders how much Ann Donne knew about
the correspondence, or how keen Bridget White, months
away from her marriage, was regarding Donne's tone. We
should also bear in mind that early modern people invariably
had a vigorous sense of humour, so the joke about London
being a 'dead carkasse' because of her absence also works as

a reflection on a city that was frequently visited by outbreaks of plague.[39] Donne's transgressive and provocative friendship may have been just what an equally robust young woman sought and desired.

Certainly the friendship endured after her marriage and we have a very different letter from Donne, written fourteen years later, to console her on the death of her husband. He reminds Lady Kingsmill to remember the admirable qualities of the deceased and to comfort herself with the thought that she cannot be a widow as she has 'willingly sacrificed' herself to God and so has become a bride of Christ.[40] Donne had more significant relationships – or, at least, ones that are more fully documented – with the aristocratic women who acted as his patrons: notably, Lucy Russell, née Harington, Countess of Bedford, and Mrs Magdalen Herbert (d. 1627), wife of Sir Edward Herbert, to whom he also wrote verse letters.[41]

The well-educated Lucy Russell could speak Spanish, Italian and French. Married to Edward Russell, 3rd Earl of Bedford (1572–1627), when she was fourteen, the couple became conspicuously important courtiers in the last years of Elizabeth's reign, a role that was restricted after the earl was significantly fined and had his freedom of movement limited after he was implicated in the Essex rebellion in 1601. Restored to favour with the accession of James, the countess became a lady of the bedchamber to Queen Anne, ran her diverse estates and, most significantly, patronized a number of important writers, including Michael Drayton, John Florio, Samuel Daniel and Ben Jonson. She was especially close to Donne from 1607 to 1615, when they fell out, and she undoubtedly wrote verse and exchanged poems with him (none has survived).[42]

Donne usually referred to the countess as his 'most affectionate friend and servant' in his letters and he reiterated the significance of their relationship when it appears to have come under pressure after Donne moved into the orbit of Sir Robert Drury, reminding her of the importance of the letter in sustaining intimacy: 'by which we deliver over our affections, and assurances of friendship, and the best faculties of our souls, times and days cannot have interest, nor be considerable, because that which passes by them, is eternal, and out of the measure of time.'[43] The relationship between the two is a complicated balancing act of patron and patronized, and two friends.

Donne addressed six verse letters to the countess, more than to any other members of his circle. The first of these, written at New Year 1607, draws attention to his inferior and supplicatory status, as well as outlining what a properly employed poet can do for a patron:

> I sum the years, and me, and find me not
>   Debtor to th' old, nor creditor to the new,
> That cannot say my thanks I have forgot,
>   Nor trust I this with hopes; and yet, scarce true
> This bravery is, since these times showed me you.
>
> In recompense, I would show future times
>   What you were, and teach them to urge towards
>   such.
> Verse embalms virtue, and tombs, or thrones of rhymes

> Preserve frail, transitory fame, as much
> As spice doth bodies from corrupt airs' touch.[44]

The poem, like many of Shakespeare's sonnets, some of which may have been written at about the same time, draws attention to the financial relationship between poet and patron, rather than denying that it was written for personal gain.[45] The speaker asserts, probably with some relief, that he is neither a borrower nor a lender, that his credit is intact: a situation, he acknowledges, which is due to the countess's help.[46] He has not forgotten to express his gratitude properly, and knows that any boast of his good fortune requires an acknowledgement of her help. Therefore, he will write a poem for her that will preserve her virtue far better than exotic spices embalm dead bodies and will act like a funeral monument.

Donne claims, with mock modesty designed for his patron and her circle, that, even so, his poem is not worthy to express the extent of her virtues:

> When all (as truth commands assent) confess
>   All truth of you, yet they will doubt how I
> (One corn of one low anthill's dust, and less)
>   Should name, know, or express a thing so high,
> And (not an inch) measure infinity. (26–30)

The second half of the poem argues that as Donne cannot express the Countess's virtues adequately she should turn to God, who will teach her how to represent herself in the best possible way and make her wise enough to understand the good and bad in others. The poem concludes with a confident assertion that her name will be among those of the saved, something that they should all celebrate at a festive time such as New Year:

From need of tears he will defend your soul,
    Or make a rebaptizing of one tear;
He cannot, (that's, he will not) disenrol
    Your name; and when with active joy we hear
This private gospel, then 'tis our New Year. (61–5)

The poem is a tour de force as a light-hearted but serious celebration. It touches on sombre, even dark, themes, and asserts the need for proper religious devotion, but ends with a joyful and extravagant compliment to the countess, that those in her company will feel uplifted and renewed when they understand that her virtue means that she will be one of the saved.

Donne undoubtedly felt proper gratitude to the Countess of Bedford, but whether he found composing such poems in her honour a strain is harder to know. He was clearly able to write them to order, as he was, later, sermons. But whether he felt that this was just part of his job, felt compromised, or had a cynical attitude to such works, we cannot really know. Donne's last two poems addressed to the countess were probably written from Germany, at at Easter 1612, where he was travelling with Sir Robert Drury and his family. Both deal with images of death in a more forceful manner than in the earlier, celebratory poem. In the first of the two poems Donne imagines himself buried in the box the countess uses to keep her letters and ends with the fantasy that both are terminally ill – possibly through self-inflicted means – and, therefore, about to witness their souls escape from their bodies and intermingle more intimately:

> Here bodies with less miracle enjoy
> Such priv'leges, enabled here to scale
> Heav'n, when the trumpet's air shall them exhale.
> Hear this and mend thyself, and thou mend'st me,
> By making me, being dead, do good for thee;
> And think me well composed, that I could now
> A last sick hour to syllables allow.[47]

Donne imagines his and the countess's souls rising to heaven on the Day of Judgement, which then makes him wish to be dangerously ill so that they can look forward to the joys of the afterlife, their earthly relationship properly 'mended' through their deaths. The second poem, which is unfinished, begins, 'Though I be dead and buried, yet I have / (Living in you) Court enough in my grave.'[48]

The lines may be read as self-regarding, centred on himself and his identity in expressing Donne's elaborate thinking about the relationship between the body and the soul and a desire to explore different possibilities. They may be insincere, reflecting the fear that he would lose his most generous patron, perhaps expressing guilt that he was travelling with another benefactor, and designed to win back her favour.[49] Or they might be read as a fitting tribute to a powerful and impressive woman he held dear and whose life and friendship he wanted to celebrate.

Chronology

1572	John Donne born (between January and June) in Bread Street, London; third of six children. Parents: John Donne (c. 1535–1576), merchant and warden of the Ironmongers' Company, and Elizabeth, née Heywood (c. 1543–1631), from a prominent Catholic family (the interlude writer, John Heywood (1496/7–c. 1578), is her father; St Thomas More (1478–1535), her great-uncle)
1576	Father dies (in January?)
	In July, mother marries Dr John Syminges, sometime president of the Royal College of Physicians
1577	Sister, Elizabeth, dies
1581	Sisters, Mary and Katherine, die in November
1584	In October, matriculates at Hart Hall, Oxford, with his brother, Henry Donne
1588	Stepfather dies in July
1588–91	Whereabouts uncertain; may be at Cambridge and may travel abroad
1590–91	Mother marries Richard Rainsford, a well-known Catholic
1591	Attends Thaives Inn
1592	Enters Lincoln's Inn in May
1593	Becomes Master of the Revels at Lincoln's Inn in February
	In June, inherits part of father's estate
1594	Brother Henry dies of plague while in Newgate Prison, imprisoned for harbouring a priest. Inherits part of brother Henry's estate in April

1596	Sails from Plymouth on the Essex–Raleigh voyage to Cadiz in June and in August returns to England
1597	Sails for Azores in July, but fleet is caught in storm and returns to Plymouth. Sails to Azores again in August but ships becalmed; returns to Plymouth in October
1597–8	Enters service of Sir Thomas Egerton, the Lord Keeper of England
1600	In lodgings near the Savoy district, south of the Strand
1601	Between October and December, becomes MP for Brackley. In December, marries Ann More, daughter of Sir George More, Egerton's brother-in-law
1602	Confesses about marriage to father-in-law in February and is imprisoned in Fleet Prison and dismissed by Egerton. In April, legality of the marriage upheld by Court of Audiences. Moves to Pyrford, Surrey, to stay with wife's cousin, Sir Francis Wolley
1603	Daughter, Constance, born
1604	Son, John, born
1605	In France and Italy; son, George, born
1606	In April, returns to England and family move to Mitcham, Surrey
1606–7	Son, Francis, born; lodging in The Strand
1606–10	Working for Thomas Morton, chaplain to Earl of Rutland, on anti-Catholic writings
1607	Morton asks Donne to become a Church of England clergyman but he declines
1608	Daughter, Lucy, born; Lucy, Countess of Bedford, becomes her godmother
1608–9	Seeks secretarial positions in Ireland and with the Virginia Company without success
1609	Daughter, Bridget, born
1610	*Pseudo-Martyr* published in January
1611	Daughter, Mary, born; *Ignatius His Conclave* published
1611–12	Travels in France and Germany with Sir Robert Drury (Ann and children stay on Isle of Wight). *The Anniversaries* published. In September 1612, family is reunited and move to house on Drury estate, Drury Lane

1613	Son, Nicholas, born
1614	In April–June, becomes MP for Taunton. Daughter, Mary, dies in May. Son, Francis, dies in November
1615	On 23 January, ordained deacon and priest at St Paul's Cathedral and appointed a royal chaplain. Daughter, Margaret, born in April. On 30 April, makes earliest surviving sermon before the queen at Greenwich
1616	Made rector at Keyston, Huntingdonshire in January Preaches to Court at Whitehall in April. Made rector at Sevenoaks, Kent, in July. Appointed reader in divinity at Lincoln's Inn in October
1617	Delivers a large number of sermons in London and the provinces. A child is still-born in August. Ann Donne dies on 15 August
1618	Preaches sermons in London
1619–21	Preaches at Court and elsewhere in London, and travels to Germany and the Low Countries to preach (May 1619–January 1620)
1621	Elected dean of St Paul's Cathedral on 22 November On 25 December, preaches Christmas Day sermon at St Paul's
1622–	Sermons regularly published
1622–3	Preaches in London and elsewhere; made Justice of the Peace for Kent and Bedfordshire; appointed Judge in Church of Delegates; made honorary member of the Virginia Company
1623	Seriously ill from November to December In December, daughter Constance marries the actor Edward Alleyn (1566–1626)
1624	*Devotions* published
1625	Conflict with Alleyn over financial matters; preaches first sermon for new king, Charles; ill (June)
1626	Daughter Constance's marriage to Alleyn breaks down
1627	Daughter Lucy dies in January. Close friend Sir Henry Goodere dies in March Patron and friend Lucy, Countess of Bedford, dies in May

	Patron and friend Lady Magdalen Herbert dies in June; Donne preaches her funeral sermon
1628	Friend Christopher Brook dies in February
1630	Daughter Constance marries Samuel Harvey in June Seriously ill in autumn. Makes will on 13 December
1631	Mother dies (aged around 86) in January. February–March: poses for drawing in his shroud. On 25 February, delivers last sermon at Court: *Death's Duell*. Dies on 31 March. Buried at St Paul's on 3 April
1632	Memorial statue erected in St Paul's
1633	First edition of *Poems* published (reprinted 1635, 1639)
1640	*LXXX Sermons* published along with life by Isaak Walton
1650	Edition of poems overseen by son, John Donne, published

REFERENCES

Preface: Donne the Thinker

1 Cited in A. J. Smith, ed., *John Donne: The Critical Heritage* (London, 1983), p. 108. I owe this point to Neil Rhodes.

2 Donne had little time for Copernicus' ideas: John Carey, *John Donne: Life, Mind and Art* (London, 1981), pp. 234–5.

3 See Gordon Teskey, 'The Metaphysics of the Metaphysicals', in *John Donne in Context*, ed. Michael Schoenfeldt (Cambridge, 2019), pp. 236–46, at p. 238.

4 T. S. Eliot, 'The Metaphysical Poets', in *Selected Essays, 3rd edn* (London, 1951), pp. 281–91, at p. 287.

5 Terry Eagleton, *Literary Theory: An Introduction* (Oxford, 1983), pp. 32–3.

6 Stevie Davies, *John Donne* (Tavistock, Devon, 1994), p. 30.

7 Ilona Bell, 'Gender Matters: The Women in Donne's Poems', in *The Cambridge Companion to John Donne*, ed. Achsah Guibbory (Cambridge, 2006), pp. 201–16; on Lawrence see Kate Millett, *Sexual Politics* (London, 1970).

8 See, for example, Simon Schama, 'John Donne', broadcast 4 September 2009: www.telegraph.co.uk (accessed 3 February 2019).

9 Schoenfeldt, 'Introduction', in Schoenfeldt, ed., *Donne in Context*, pp. 1–4, at p. 1.

10 John Donne, *The Oxford Edition of the Sermons of John Donne*, ed. Peter McCullough et al. (Oxford, 2013–).

11 For a recent relevant argument see Gordon Teskey, *Spenserian Moments* (Cambridge, MA, 2019).

12 Rather like Milton: see Stephen B. Dobranski and John
    P. Rumrich, eds, *Milton and Heresy* (Cambridge, 2009).

1 The Soul and the Self

1   Tarnya Cooper, *Citizen Portrait: Portrait Painting and the Urban Elite of
    Tudor and Jacobean England and Wales* (New Haven, CT, 2012), p. 176.
2   Ibid., p. 177; Jonathan F. S. Post, 'Donne's Life: A Sketch', in
    The Cambridge Companion to John Donne, ed. Achsah Guibbory
    (Cambridge, 2006), pp. 1–22, at p. 6.
3   Ramie Targoff, *John Donne: Body and Soul* (Chicago, IL, 2008).
4   This is a biographical study of Donne which concentrates on
    how religion shaped his identity; the definitive study of Donne's
    thinking about religion will be Shanyn Altman's *Martyrdom in
    John Donne's England: Absolutism, Conformity and Cases of Conscience*
    (Manchester, forthcoming). See also Altman, '"An Anxious
    Entangling and Perplexing of Conciences": John Donne and
    Catholic Recusant Mendacity', in *Mendacity in Early Modern
    Literature and Culture*, ed. Ingo Berensmeyer and Andrew Hadfield
    (Abingdon, 2016), pp. 46–58.
5   For an overview explaining how the study of the Reformation has
    changed see Christopher Haigh, 'A. G. Dickens and the English
    Reformation', *Historical Research*, 77 (2004), pp. 24–38.
6   S. J. Barnett, 'Where Was Your Church before Luther? Claims for
    Antiquity of Protestantism Examined', *Church History*, 68 (1999),
    pp. 14–41.
7   Andrew Hadfield, *Lying in Early Modern English Culture from the Oath
    of Supremacy to the Oath of Allegiance* (Oxford, 2017), p. 124.
8   Diarmaid MacCulloch, 'A House Divided (1517–1660)',
    in *A History of Christianity* (London, 2009), pp. 604–54.
9   John Donne, *The Complete Poems of John Donne*, ed. Robin Robbins
    (Harlow, 2008), p. 547. All subsequent references here are to this
    edition.
10 For Donne's analysis of the origin of the soul see Targoff, *Body and
    Soul*, pp. xxvi–xxxv.
11 Most powerfully expressed in John Carey, *John Donne: Life, Mind
    and Art* (London, 1981), esp. p. xi, but this reading of Donne is

in Walton's life (1640) and in the first modern biography, Edmund Gosse's *The Life and Letters of John Donne*, 2 vols (London, 1899). Donne does occasionally reinforce this understanding of his life in his letters: see John Donne, *Selected Letters*, ed. P. M. Oliver (New York, 2002), pp. 88–9. For an understanding of how Donne's life was constructed problematically by his published work see David Scott Kastan, 'The Body of the Text', ELH, 81 (2014), pp. 443–67.

12 Eamon Duffy, *The Stripping of the Altars: Traditional Religion in England, 1400–1580* (New Haven, CT, 1992), pp. 384–5.

13 See Andrew Hadfield, 'How to Read Nashe's "Brightness Falls from the Air"', *Forum for Modern Language Studies*, 51 (2015), pp. 239–47.

14 Alan Stewart, *The Cradle King: A Life of James VI and I* (London, 2004), p. 195.

15 Patricia Badir, *The Maudlin Impression: English Literary Images of Mary Magdalene, 1550–1700* (Notre Dame, IN, 2009), esp. pp. 6, 27–8, 155–7.

16 Donne, *Complete Poems*, ed. Robbins, p. 149; R. C. Bald, *John Donne: A Life* (Oxford, 1970), p. 144. See below, ch. 4.

17 See the related argument in Gregory Kneidel, 'Donne and the Virtue of Religion', *Religion and Literature*, 46 (2019), pp. 50–60.

18 Thomas Arnold, *The Renaissance at War* (London, 2001), pp. 60–67.

19 William Whately, *A Bride-bush; or, A Wedding Sermon Compendiously Describing the Duties of Married Persons* (London, 1617), p. 2.

20 Robert S. Miola, ed., *Early Modern Catholicism: An Anthology of Primary Sources* (Oxford, 2007), pp. 7–8; Alison Shell, *Catholicism, Controversy and the English Literary Imagination, 1558–1660* (Cambridge, 1999), esp. pp. 11, 60, 80.

21 Alan Stewart, *The Oxford History of Life-writing*, vol. II: *Early Modern* (Oxford, 2018), p. 222.

22 Jerry Brotton, *A History of the World in Twelve Maps* (London, 2012), pp. 186–259.

23 See Margaret T. Hodgen, *Early Anthropology in the Sixteenth and Seventeenth Centuries* (Philadelphia, PA, 1964), pp. 207–53.

24 John Donne, *Paradoxes and Problems*, ed. Helen Peters (Oxford, 1980), Introduction, pp. xxvi–ii. Subsequent references are to this edition and are given in parentheses in the text.

25 Eric Langley, *Narcissism and Suicide in Shakespeare and His Contemporaries* (Oxford, 2009), p. 218.

26 F. L. Cross and E. A. Livingstone, eds, *The Oxford Dictionary of the Christian Church* (Oxford, 1997), 3rd edn, pp. 1566–7; Jeffrey R. Watt, 'Calvin on Suicide', *Church History*, 66 (1997), pp. 463–76.

27 Brian Cummings, *Mortal Thoughts: Religion, Secularity and Identity in Shakespeare and Early Modern Culture* (Oxford, 2013), p. 272; Uwe Michael Lang, 'Augustine's Conception of Sacrifice in *City of God*, Book X, and the Eucharistic Sacrifice', *Antiphon: A Journal for Liturgical Renewal*, 19 (2015), pp. 29–51.

28 John Donne, *Biathanatos*, in *Selected Prose*, ed. Neil Rhodes (Harmondsworth, 1987, rev. 2015), pp. 59–85, at p. 71. For a full discussion of Donne, suicide and martyrdom see Altman, *Martyrdom*, ch. 4.

29 Carlos M. N. Eire, *War against the Idols: The Reformation of Worship from Erasmus to Calvin* (Cambridge, 1986).

30 A. E. Malloch, 'Father Henry Garnet's Treatise of Equivocation', *Recusant History*, 15 (1981), pp. 387–95; Hadfield, *Lying*, pp. 90–93.

31 Peter Iver Kaufman, *Prayer, Despair and Drama* (Urbana, IL, 1996).

32 *The Oxford Edition of the Sermons of John Donne*, vol. III: *Sermons Preached at the Court of Charles I*, ed. David Colclough (Oxford, 2013), pp. 229–46. Subsequent references to this sermon appear as bracketed page numbers and refer to this edition. For a sustained analysis see Targoff, *Body and Soul*, ch. 6.

33 *The Oxford Edition of the Sermons*, vol. III, p. 247.

34 Henry King [?], 'An Elegy on Dr. Donne, Deane of Pauls', in *The Oxford Edition of the Sermons*, vol. III, p. 248.

35 Marginal note, *Exitus a morte vteri*, 'the issue from the death of the womb'.

36 *The Book of Common Prayer: The Texts of 1549, 1559, and 1662*, ed. Brian Cummings (Oxford, 2011), Introduction, p. lii.

37 See Targoff, *Body and Soul*, pp. 8–9.

38 Andrew Cunningham and Ole Peter Grell, *The Four Horsemen of the Apocalypse: Religion, War, Famine and Death in Reformation Europe* (Cambridge, 2000); Guido Alfani, *Calamities and the Economy in Renaissance Italy: The Grand Tour of the Horsemen of the Apocalypse*, trans. Christine Calvert (Basingstoke, 2013).

39 George Herbert, 'Death', lines 1–8, in *The English Poems of George Herbert*, ed. Helen Wilcox (Cambridge, 2007), pp. 647–9. Herbert's poem was probably written not long after Donne's and, as they did exchange poems, it is possible that Herbert had seen Donne's sonnet: Bald, *A Life*, pp. 305–6. On Donne's friendship with Herbert see also David Novarr, *The Disinterred Muse: Donne's Texts and Contexts* (Ithaca, NY, 1980), pp. 105–7.

40 On Donne and the desire for death see Jacques Derrida, *The Beast and the Sovereign*, vol. II, trans. Geoff Bennington (Chicago, IL, 2011), pp. 50–53.

2 Religion

1 David Colclough, 'Donne, John', *Oxford Dictionary of National Biography*, https://doi.org/10.1093/ref:odnb/7819.

2 John Stubbs, *Donne: The Reformed Soul* (London, 2006), pp. 70–71.

3 William P. Haugaard, *Elizabeth and the English Reformation* (Cambridge, 1968), pp. 247–72.

4 Dennis Flynn, *John Donne and the Ancient Catholic Nobility* (Bloomington, IN, 1995), pp. 131–46.

5 R. C. Bald, *John Donne: A Life* (Oxford, 1970), p. 58.

6 John Carey, *John Donne: Life, Mind and Art* (London, 1981), p. 11.

7 David Novarr, *The Disinterred Muse: Donne's Texts and Contexts* (Ithaca, NY, 1980), p. 95.

8 John Donne, *Selected Letters*, ed. P. M. Oliver (New York, 2002), pp. 8–11.

9 See ch. 4.

10 Eighty-two copies survive which would appear to indicate a large print run (although it may have been carefully targeted at a Catholic audience rather than being for the general reader): John Donne, *Pseudo-Martyr*, ed. Anthony Raspa (Montreal and Kingston, 1993), Introduction, p. xxxv.

11 For analysis see Anne Lake Prescott, 'Menippean Donne', in *The Oxford Handbook of John Donne*, ed. Jeanne Shami, Dennis Flynn and M. Thomas Hester (Oxford, 2011), pp. 158–79, at pp. 168–73.

12 See ch. 1.

13 See ch. 1.

14 Arnold Pritchard, *Catholic Loyalism in Elizabethan England* (London, 1979); Michael C. Questier, *Catholicism and Community in Early Modern England: Politics, Aristocratic Patronage and Religion, c. 1550–1640* (Cambridge, 2006), pp. 288–314; Peter Lake and Michael Questier, *All Hail to the Archpriest: Confessional Conflict, Toleration, and the Politics of Publicity in Post-Reformation England* (Oxford, 2019), esp. pp. 111–17.

15 David Wootton, 'John Donne's Religion of Love,' in *Heterodoxy in Early Modern Science and Religion*, ed. John Brooke and Ian MacLean (Oxford, 2005), pp. 31–80. On 'mortalism' see ch. 1.

16 For one powerful argument see Eamon Duffy, *Fires of Faith: Catholic England under Mary Tudor* (New Haven, CT, 2009).

17 Alexandra Walsham, *Church Papists: Catholicism, Conformity and Confessional Polemic in Early Modern England* (Woodbridge, 1993); David Scott Kastan, *A Will to Believe: Shakespeare and Religion* (Oxford, 2014), ch. 1; Lake and Questier, *All Hail the Archpriest*, p. 14.

18 On the pivotal significance of *Pseudo-Martyr* in Donne's thinking see Shanyn Altman, *Martyrdom in John Donne's England: Absolutism, Conformity and Cases of Conscience* (Manchester, forthcoming).

19 On the plot see Mark Nicholls, *Investigating Gunpowder Plot* (Manchester, 1991). On the plot's significance in European culture see Robert Appelbaum, *Terrorism before the Letter: Mythography and Political Violence in England, Scotland, and France, 1559–1642* (Oxford, 2015), pp. 54–6.

20 Clarence J. Ryan, 'The Jacobean Oath of Allegiance and English Lay Catholics', *Catholic Historical Review*, 28 (1942), pp. 159–83; Michael C. Questier, 'Loyalty, Religion and State Power in Early Modern England: English Romanism and the Jacobean Oath of Allegiance', *Historical Journal*, 40 (1997), pp. 311–29.

21 James VI and I, *The Trew Law of Free Monarchies* in *Political Writings*, ed. Johann P. Sommerville (Cambridge, 1994), pp. 62–84.

22 Donne, *Pseudo-Martyr*, ed. Raspa, introduction, p. xxxv. All subsequent references to this edition are in parentheses in the text. Some sections in the next few paragraphs have been adapted from my essay, 'Chapter Twenty Four: Controversial Prose', in Michael Schoenfeldt, ed., *John Donne in Context* (Cambridge, 2019), pp. 247–55.

23   Donne, *Pseudo-Martyr*, esp. pp. 9, 160–62.

24   Jonathan Michael Gray, *Oaths and the English Reformation* (Cambridge, 2013); John Kerrigan, *Shakespeare's Binding Language* (Oxford, 2016).

25   David Nicholls, 'The Political Theology of John Donne', *Theological Studies*, 49 (1988), pp. 45–66, p. 65.

26   David Novarr argues that Donne stopped writing verse after he was ordained, only producing occasional poems when requested to do so. His literary sensibilities were absorbed into his new role as a preacher because 'the sermons multiply his exploration of possibilities, his recognition of alternatives, his invention of ingenuities because he had arrived at settled convictions about the relationship between man and God': *Disinterred Muse*, p. 99.

27   C. A. Patrides and Joseph Wittreich, eds, *The Apocalypse in English Renaissance Thought and Literature* (Manchester, 1984). See also ch. 1.

28   Howard Marchitello, *The Machine in the Text: Science and Literature in the Age of Shakespeare and Galileo* (Oxford, 2011), ch. 5.

29   See ch. 1.

30   John Stachniewski, 'John Donne: The Despair of the "Holy Sonnets"', *ELH*, 48 (1981), pp. 677–705. On 'double predestination' see R. T. Kendall, *Calvin and English Calvinism to 1649* (Oxford, 1979), pp. 198–9.

31   On Donne's animated responses to visual culture see Ann Hurley, *John Donne's Poetry and Early Modern Visual Culture* (Selinsgrove, PA, 2005).

32   Hannibal Hamlin, *Psalm Culture and Early Modern English Literature* (Cambridge, 2004), ch. 6. Donne preached four sermons on the penitential psalms at St Paul's Cathedral in 1626: *The Oxford Edition of the Sermons of John Donne: XII, Sermons Preached at St Paul's Cathedral, 1626*, ed. Mary Ann Lund (Oxford, 2017), pp. 3–66.

33   Thomas Sternhold, John Hopkins and William Whittingham, *The Whole Booke of Psalmes, Collected into Englishe Metre* (London, 1584), pp. 147–8.

34   John N. King, *Foxe's 'Book of Martyrs' and Early Modern Print Culture* (Cambridge, 2006), pp. 37–41.

35   John Donne, *The Complete Poems of John Donne*, ed. Robin Robbins (Harlow, 2008), p. 392.

36 Juvenal, *The Sixteen Satires*, trans. Peter Green (Harmondsworth, 1967), pp. 79–81.

37 See ch. 1.

38 Katrin Ettenhuber, *Donne's Augustine: Renaissance Cultures of Interpretation* (Oxford, 2011), pp. 2–3.

39 Debora Shuger, 'Donne's Absolutism', in *Oxford Handbook of John Donne*, ed. Shami et al., pp. 690–703.

40 Francis Oakley, 'Christian Obedience and Authority, 1520–1550', in *The Cambridge History of Political Thought, 1450–1700*, ed. J. H. Burns and Mark Goldie (Cambridge, 1991), pp. 159–92, at pp. 163–75.

41 Gerard Kilroy, *Edmund Campion: A Scholarly Life* (Farnham, 2015), ch. 10.

42 Roy W. Battenhouse, 'The Grounds of Religious Toleration in the Thought of John Donne', *Church History*, 11 (1942), pp. 217–48; Achsah Guibbory, *Returning to John Donne* (Abingdon, 2015), pp. 229–62.

43 *The Collected Sermons of John Donne*, ed. George Potter and Evelyn Simpson, 10 vols (Berkeley, CA, 1953–62), vol. VIII, pp. 219–36, at p. 219.

44 There is a possible allusion to Luther's concept of *Posteriora Dei*, the notion that we can only see God from the rear: see George L. Murphy, *The Cosmos in the Light of the Cross* (London, 2003), p. 36. I owe this point to Shanyn Altman.

45 Klaas van Berkel and Arie Johan Vanderjagt, eds, *The Book of Nature in Early Modern and Modern History* (Leuven, 2006).

46 *The Oxford Edition of the Sermons of John Donne*, vol. III: *Sermons Preached at the Court of Charles I*, ed. David Colclough (Oxford, 2013), pp. 39–55.

47 For details see Bald, *A Life*, pp. 237–62.

48 Stephen Shapin, *The Scientific Revolution* (Chicago, IL, 1996), p. 28.

3 Sexuality

1 On Donne as a 'metaphysical' poet see ch. 6.

2 See ch. 2 above.

3 Sasha Roberts, *Reading Shakespeare's Poems in Early Modern England* (Basingstoke, 2001); *The Three Parnassus Plays*, ed. J. B. Leishman (London, 1949), Introduction, pp. 55–6.

4 David Riggs, *The World of Christopher Marlowe* (London, 2004), ch. 5.

5 *The Works of Thomas Nashe*, ed. R. B. McKerrow, rev. F. P. Wilson, 5 vols (Oxford, 1958), vol. III, pp. 397–416.

6 Lauren Silberman, *Transforming Desire: Erotic Knowledge in Books III and IV of The Faerie Queene* (Berkeley, CA, 1995).

7 Barnes became notorious for the lines, 'Or that sweet wine, which downe her throate doth trickle, / To kisse her lippes, and lye next at her hart, / Runne through her vaynes, and passe by pleasures part': Barnabe Barnes, *Parthenophil and Parthenophe* (London, 1593), Sonnet 63. The conceit was ridiculed by other writers, notably in Thomas Campion's Latin Epigram 17, 'In Barnum': 'In vinum solvi cupis Auflena haurit, / Basia sic felix, dum bibit illa, dabis / Forsitan attinges quoque cor; sed (Barne) matella, / Exceptus tandem, quails amator eris?' ('You want to be dissolved in the wine which Auflena drinks; thus you will happily kiss her while she is drinking; perhaps you will touch her heart too; but, Barnes, after you are caught in the chamber pot, what a lover you will be!': *The Works of Thomas Campion: Complete Songs, Masques, and Treatises with a Selection of the Latin*, ed. Walter R. Davis (New York, 1967), p. 409.

8 See ch. 2 above.

9 *Songs and Sonnets* first appears as a title of a section in the second edition of Donne's poems (1639) so is almost certainly not authorial, something of an irony given its fame and Donne's preference for circulating his work in manuscript rather than print.

10 On the date see John Donne, *The Complete Poems of John Donne*, ed. Robin Robbins (Harlow, 2008), p. 253. On the Countess see Helen Payne, 'Russell [née Harington], Lucy, Countess of Bedford', *Oxford Dictionary of National Biography*, www.oxforddnb.com, hereafter ODNB. On her patronage of Donne see R. C. Bald, *John Donne: A Life* (Oxford, 1970), pp. 172–80, 274–6, 294–7.

11 See ch. 5 below.

12 Linda Woodbridge, *Women and the English Renaissance: Literature and the Nature of Womankind, 1540–1620* (Urbana, IL, 1986), p. 35.

13 See ch. 2 below.

14 For a different reading see John Carey, *John Donne: Life, Mind and Art* (London, 1981), pp. 64–6.

15 Arthur F. Marotti, *John Donne, Coterie Poet* (Madison, WI, 1986);
    Daniel Starza Smith, *John Donne and the Conway Papers: Patronage and
    Manuscript Circulation in the Early Seventeenth Century* (Oxford, 2014).

16 Ovid, Book 1, Elegy 5, in *Amores*, trans. Guy Lee (London, 1968),
    lines 13–26 (pp. 15–17).

17 Sir Philip Sidney, *An Apology for Poetry*, ed. Geoffrey Shepherd,
    rev. R. W. Maslen (Manchester, 2002), pp. 110–13.

18 Donne, *Complete Poems*, ed. Robbins, p. 325.

19 For an overview see Ian Frederick Moulton, *Before Pornography: Erotic
    Writing in Early Modern England* (Oxford, 2000).

20 William Shakespeare, *Venus and Adonis*, lines 229–40, in *The Poems*,
    ed. F. T. Prince (London, 1998), pp. 16–17.

21 Anthony Mortimer, *Variable Passions: A Reading of Shakespeare's 'Venus
    and Adonis'* (New York, 2000).

22 Charles Nicholl, *A Cup of News: The Life of Thomas Nashe* (London,
    1984), pp. 89–90.

23 Nashe, 'The Choise of Valentines', lines 106–20, in *Works*, vol. III,
    pp. 408–9.

24 Ovid, Book 3, Elegy 7.

25 Matthew Dimmock, *Mythologies of the Prophet Muhammad in Early
    Modern English Culture* (Cambridge, 2013), p. 30.

26 See Bald, *A Life*, pp. 80–85, 90–93.

27 See Joan Pong Linton, *The Romance of the New World: Gender and the
    Literary Formations of English Colonialism* (Cambridge, 1998), pp. 39–61.

28 Louis A. Montrose, 'The Work of Gender in the Discourse of
    Discovery', *Representations*, 33 (1991), pp. 1–41.

29 Sir Walter Raleigh, *The Discoverie of the Large, Rich and Bewtiful Empyre
    of Guiana*, ed. Neil L. Whitehead (Manchester, 1997), p. 196. See
    also Charles Nicholl, *The Creature in the Map: A Journey to El Dorado*
    (London, 1995).

30 Anna Beer, *Bess: The Life of Lady Raleigh, Wife to Sir Walter* (London,
    2004), pp. 57–76.

31 Andrew Hadfield, *Literature, Travel and Colonialism in the English
    Renaissance, 1540–1625* (Oxford, 1998), pp. 70–111.

32 Gordon Williams, *A Dictionary of Sexual Language and Imagery in
    Shakespearean and Stuart Literature*, 3 vols (London, 1994), vol. I,
    pp. 324–5.

33 Ernst Cassirer, Paul Oskar Kristeller and John Herman Randall, Jr, eds, *The Renaissance Philosophy of Man* (Chicago, IL, 1948). For discussions of Donne see, for example, the influential works by Rosamund Tuve, *Elizabethan and Metaphysical Imagery* (Chicago, IL, 1947), p. 41; Helen Gardner, 'The Argument about "The Ecstasy"', in *Elizabethan and Jacobean Studies Presented to Frank Percy Wilson*, ed. Herbert David and Helen Gardner (Oxford, 1959), pp. 279–306. A more nuanced and sophisticated analysis is provided in Melissa Sanchez, 'Elegies and Satires', in *John Donne in Context*, ed. Michael Schoenfeldt (Cambridge, 2019), pp. 58–67.

34 See Ramie Targoff, *John Donne: Body and Soul* (Chicago, IL, 2008), p. 62.

35 Kathleen M. Llewellyn, 'Deadly Sex and Sexy Death in Early Modern French Literature', in *Sexuality in the Middle Ages and Early Modern Times: New Approaches to a Fundamental Cultural-historical and Literary-anthropological Theme*, ed. Albrecht Classen (Berlin, 2008), pp. 811–36.

36 Anne Laurence, *Women in England, 1500–1700: A Social History* (London, 1994), p. 65; Ian Maclean, *The Renaissance Notion of Woman: A Study of the Fortunes of Scholasticism and Medical Science in European Intellectual Life* (Oxford, 1980), p. 105.

37 On this last point see Martin Ingram, *Church Courts, Sex and Marriage in England, 1570–1640* (Cambridge, 1990).

38 Ovid, *Metamorphoses*, trans. Mary M. Innes (Harmondsworth, 1955), pp. 240–44.

39 H. David Brumble, *Classical Myths and Legends in the Middle Ages and Renaissance: A Dictionary of Allegorical Meanings* (London, 1998), pp. 39–40.

40 Ovid, Elegy 11b, Book 3.

41 *The Book of Common Prayer: The Texts of 1549, 1559, and 1662*, ed. Brian Cummings (Oxford, 2011), p. 64.

42 Donne, *Complete Poems*, ed. Robbins, p. 169.

43 See, for example, Wilbur Sanders, *John Donne's Poetry* (Cambridge, 1971), p. 99; David Novarr, *The Disinterred Muse: Donne's Texts and Contexts* (Ithaca, NY, 1980), pp. 17–39; Carey, *Donne*, pp. 252–5.

44 See Brian Vickers, ed., *English Renaissance Literary Criticism* (Oxford, 1999), esp. pp. 179–89.

45 John Milton, *Paradise Lost*, ed. Alastair Fowler (Harlow, 1968), Book 8, lines 618–19, 622–9.

46 Barbara Lewalski, *The Life of John Milton* (Oxford, 2000), p. 6.

47 On Spenser and Neoplatonism see Kenneth Borris, *Visionary Spenser and the Poetics of Early Modern Platonism* (Oxford, 2017).

48 C. S. Lewis, *The Allegory of Love: A Study in Medieval Tradition* [1936] (Oxford, 1979), p. 340.

4 Marriage

1 David Cressy, *Birth, Marriage and Death: Ritual, Religion, and the Life-cycle in Tudor and Stuart England* (Oxford, 1997), ch. 12–16.

2 Peter Searby, *A History of the University of Cambridge: 1750–1870* (Cambridge, 1988), Introduction, p. 6.

3 Archie Armstrong, *A Choice Banquet of Witty Jests, Rare Fancies, and Pleasant Novels Fitted for All the Lovers of Wit, Mirth and Eloquence* (London, 1660), p. 72; John Stubbs, *Donne: The Reformed Soul* (London, 2006), p. 154.

4 John Donne to Sir George More, 2 February 1602, in John Donne, *Selected Letters*, ed. P. M. Oliver (New York, 2002), pp. 10–12.

5 Jeffrey L. Singman, *Daily Life in Elizabethan England* (Westport, CT, 1995), p. 89.

6 On the Bishops' Ban see Richard A. McCabe, 'Elizabethan Satire and the Bishops' Ban of 1599', *Yearbook of English Studies*, 11 (1981), pp. 188–93. More generally see also Ian Frederick Moulton, *Before Pornography: Erotic Writing in Early Modern England* (Oxford, 2000).

7 R. C. Bald, *John Donne: A Life* (Oxford, 1970), pp. 72–3, 119–23; G. H. Martin, 'Baker, Sir Richard', A. J. Loomie, 'Wotton, Sir Henry', ODNB.

8 Richard Baker, *A Chronicle of the Kings of England* (London, 1643), p. 156.

9 Bald, *A Life*, pp. 11–15; Isaak Walton, 'The Life of Dr John Donne', in *The Lives of John Donne, Sir Henry Wotton, Richard Hooker, George Herbert, Robert Sanderson* (Oxford, 1927), pp. 8–90, at pp. 23–6.

10 Donne, *Selected Letters*, pp. 88–9.

11 Arthur F. Marotti, *John Donne, Coterie Poet* (Madison, WI, 1986). For recent discoveries see Daniel Starza Smith, Matthew Payne and

Melanie Marshall, 'Rediscovering John Donne's *Catalogus Librorum Satyricus*', *Review of English Studies*, 69 (2018), pp. 455–87; Alison Flood, 'Unknown John Donne Manuscript Discovered in Suffolk', *The Guardian*, 30 November 2018, www.theguardian.com.

12   Michael Drayton, *Poly-Olbion* (London, 1622), 'Song 21', lines 177–82, in *The Complete Works of Michael Drayton*, ed. Richard Hooper, 5 vols (London, 1876), vol. III, p. 31; Andrew Hadfield, 'Michael Drayton's Brilliant Career', *Proceedings of the British Academy*, 125 (2004), pp. 119–47, pp. 133–4.

13   *Poems by J. D. with Elegies on the Authors Death* (London, 1635). The first edition of 1633 opened with 'The Progress of the Soul'.

14   John Donne, *The Complete Poems of John Donne*, ed. Robin Robbins (Harlow, 2008), pp. 188–9.

15   James Winny, *A Preface to Donne* (London, 1970), pp. 126–8; Thomas Docherty, *John Donne, Undone* (London, 1986), pp. 53–9. Some sections of the next few paragraphs are taken from my essay, 'Donne's *Songs and Sonnets* and Artistic Identity', in Patrick Cheney, Andrew Hadfield and Garrett Sullivan, eds, *Early Modern English Poetry: A Critical Companion* (Oxford, 2006), pp. 206–16.

16   Murray Roston, *The Soul of Wit: A Study of John Donne* (Oxford, 1974), p. 109. 'Flea' poems have a particular potency in French, enabling the poet to activate a pun on *puce* (flea) and *pucelle* (virgin, maiden): Anne Lake Prescott, *French Poets and the English Renaissance: Studies in Fame and Transformation* (New Haven, CT, 1978), p. 115; Kendell B. Tarte, *Writing Places: Sixteenth-century City Culture and the Des Roches Salon* (Newark, NJ, 2007), pp. 53–6.

17   Tilottama Rajan, '"Nothing Sooner Broke": Donne's *Songs and Sonnets* as Self-consuming Artefacts', in *John Donne: Contemporary Critical Essays*, ed. Andrew Mousley (Basingstoke, 1999), pp. 45–62, at p. 57.

18   See ch. 2 above.

19   Ovid, *Amores*, trans. Guy Lee (London, 1968), 1.13 (pp. 46–7). Tithonus, Aurora's husband, was granted eternal life but not eternal youth so begged for death; Memmon was her son, an Ethiopian warrior killed by Achilles in the Trojan War. Birds visited his tomb every year.

20   Wendy Beth Hyman, *Impossible Desire and the Limits of Knowledge in Renaissance Poetry* (Oxford, 2019).

21 See Duncan Salkeld, *Madness and Drama in the Age of Shakespeare* (Manchester, 1993), pp. 11–20.

22 Alan Stewart, *The Cradle King: A Life of James VI and I* (London, 2003), pp. 176–81.

23 Barbara L. Estrin, *Laura: Uncovering Gender and Genre in Wyatt, Donne, and Marvell* (Durham, NC, 1994), pp. 147–223. See also ch. 5 below.

24 Ann Rosalind Jones and Peter Stallybrass, 'The Politics of *Astrophil and Stella*', *Studies in English Literature, 1500–1900*, 24 (1984), pp. 53–68. See also ch. 5 below.

25 Catherine Bates, 'Synecdochic Structures in the Sonnet Sequences of Sidney and Spenser', in *A Companion to Renaissance Poetry*, ed. Catherine Bates (Oxford, 2018), pp. 276–88, at p. 282.

26 On Elizabeth compared to the sun see Helen Hackett, *Virgin Mother, Maiden Queen: Elizabeth I and the Cult of the Virgin Mary* (Basingstoke, 1995), pp. 95, 113, 133, 139–40.

27 H. L. Meakin, *John Donne's Articulations of the Feminine* (Oxford, 1998), pp. 85–101.

28 *Poems by J. D.* (1633 edn), p. 202; BL Stowe MS 961, f.60r–v.

29 Bald, *A Life*, p. 144; Donne, *Complete Poems*, ed. Robbins, p. 149.

30 Lee A. Sonnino, *A Handbook to Sixteenth-century Rhetoric* (London, 1968), p. 135.

31 Evans, ed., *Elizabethan Sonnets*, p. 14. On Sidney and Penelope Devereux see Katherine Duncan-Jones, *Sir Philip Sidney: Courtier Poet* (London, 1991), pp. 196–201, 242–7.

32 Don Cameron Allen, 'John Donne's Knowledge of Renaissance Medicine', *Journal of English and Germanic Philology*, 42 (1943), pp. 322–42.

33 'Desdemona: 'I hope my noble lord esteems me honest.' / Othello: O, ay, as summer flies are in the shambles, / That quicken even with blowing.': William Shakespeare, *Othello*, ed. E.A.J. Honigmann (London, 1997), 4.2.66–8 (p. 277).

34 Donne, *Complete Poems*, ed. Robbins, p. 151.

35 Juan Luis Vives, *The Office and Duetie of an Husband* (London, 1555), C7v.

36 Cleanth Brooks, *The Well-wrought Urn: Studies in the Structure of Poetry* (New York, 1947).

37 It is notable that neither of Donne's relatively recent biographers, R. C. Bald and John Stubbs, provide much comment on the poem

or read it in biographical terms. The poem is sometimes thought to have been written when Lucy, Countess of Bedford, Donne's patron, was dangerously ill: Donne, *Complete Poems*, ed. Robbins, pp. 225–6. Readings that support the traditional understanding that the poem was composed after the death of Ann Donne include John Carey, *John Donne: Life, Mind and Art* (London, 1981), p. 78; Anthony Low, *The Reinvention of Love: Poetry, Politics and Culture from Sidney to Milton* (Cambridge, 1993), pp. 58–9; Achsah Guibbory, 'Erotic Poetry', in *The Cambridge Companion to John Donne*, ed. Achsah Guibbory (Cambridge, 2006), pp. 133–47, at p. 146.

38 See ch. 2 above. On the use of alchemical imagery see Lyndy Abraham, *A Dictionary of Alchemical Imagery* (Cambridge, 1998), p. 118 ('limbeck'); pp. 33–4 ('chaos'); pp. 187–8 ('souls'); p. 69 ('elixir'); p. 182 ('shadow').

39 Donne, *Complete Poems*, ed. Robbins, p. 273.

40 See Roy Booth, 'John Donne: Ideating Nothing', *English*, 37 (1988), pp. 203–15.

41 *The Book of Common Prayer: The Texts of 1549, 1559, and 1662*, ed. Brian Cummings (Oxford, 2011), p. 159.

42 Hobbes, 'King, Henry', ODNB.

43 Bald, *A Life*, esp. pp. 398–9, 531–3.

44 'The Exequy', in *The English Poems of Henry King*, ed. Lawrence Mason (New Haven, CT, 1914), pp. 51–5 (lines 11–29).

45 Julia Kristeva, *Black Sun: Depression and Melancholia*, trans. Leon S. Roudiez (New York, 1987).

46 See ch. 2 above.

47 M. Thomas Hester, '"Miserrimum Dictu": Donne's Epitaph for His Wife', *Journal of English and Germanic Philology*, 94 (1995), pp. 513–29.

48 Hester, '"Miserrimum Dictu"', pp. 517–18; LUNA: Folger Digital Image Collection. See also Ramie Targoff, *John Donne: Body and Soul* (Chicago, IL, 2008), pp. 92–3.

5 Learning

1 See Hugh Adlington, *John Donne's Books: Reading, Writing, and the Uses of Knowledge* (Oxford, forthcoming). Geoffrey Keynes catalogues 219 books owned by Donne: *A Bibliography of Dr John Donne, Dean of*

St Paul's [1958] (Cambridge, 1998), appendix 4, pp. 204–22 (many survive in the library of the Middle Temple); Ramie Targoff, *John Donne: Body and Soul* (Chicago, IL, 2008), p. 290. Most of Donne's books are works of theology and Greek and Latin literature, but his reading was clearly not restricted to these subjects.

2 Lawrence Manley, *Literature and Culture in Early Modern London* (Cambridge, 1995), ch. 7.

3 Wesley Trimpi, *Ben Jonson's Poems: A Study of the Plain Style* (Stanford, CA, 1962).

4 Ben Jonson, 'On My First Daughter', lines 11–12, in *The Cambridge Edition of the Works of Ben Jonson*, ed. David Bevington, Martin Butler and Ian Donaldson, 7 vols (Cambridge, 2012), vol. V, pp. 122–3; *The Poems of Catullus*, trans. Peter Whigham (Harmondsworth, 1966), p. 55.

5 Jonson, 'On My First Daughter', lines 11–12; Martial, *The Epigrams*, trans. James Michie (Harmondsworth, 1978), p. 89.

6 Jonson, *Works*, vol. V, pp. 123–4.

7 Catherine Keane, 'Defining the Art of Blame: Classical Satire', in Ruben Quintero, ed., *A Companion to Satire* (Oxford, 2007), pp. 31–52, at pp. 44–6.

8 Juvenal, Satire 2, lines 1–4, in *The Sixteen Satires*, trans. Peter Green (Harmondsworth, 1967), p. 75.

9 'Satyre I', lines 1–6, in Donne, *Complete Poems*, ed. Robbins, pp. 365–75.

10 Grand tours were often about sowing wild oats as well as becoming more cultured and networking: see Ian Littlewood, *Sultry Climates: Travel and Sex Since the Grand Tour* (London, 2001).

11 For discussion of Donne's uneasy relationship to Petrarchism see Heather Dubrow, *Echoes of Desire: English Petrarchism and Its Counterdiscourses* (Ithaca, NY, 1995), ch. 6.

12 On Petrarch see Christopher S. Celenza, *Petratrch: Everywhere a Wanderer* (London, 2017).

13 See *Petrarch's Lyric Poems: The Rime Sparse and Other Lyrics*, trans. Robert M. Durling (Cambridge, MA, 1976).

14 Petrarch, *Selections from The Canzoniere and Other Works*, trans. Mark Musa (Oxford, 1985), *Canzoniere* 190.

15 Sir Philip Sidney, *Astrophil and Stella*, in *Elizabethan Sonnets*, ed.
    Maurice Evans (London, 1977), pp. 2–61.

16 Sir John Davies, 'Gullinge Sonnets' (*c.* 1594), in *Elizabethan Sonnets*,
    ed. Evans, pp. 179–83, at p. 180.

17 Achsah Guibbory, '"Oh Let Mee Not Serve So": The Politics of
    Love in Donne's *Elegies*', *ELH*, 57 (1990), pp. 811–33.

18 Donne, 'Go and Catch a Falling Star', lines 10–18, in *Complete
    Poems*, ed. Robbins, pp. 193–6.

19 Alice S. Miskimin, *The Renaissance Chaucer* (New Haven, CT, 1975).

20 Donne, 'Woman's Constancy', lines 1–2, in *Complete Poems*, ed.
    Robbins, pp. 282–3.

21 W. B. Patterson, *King James VI and I and the Reunion of Christendom*
    (Cambridge, 1997), ch. 1.

22 See ch. 2 above.

23 On the significance of swearing oaths in the period see Jonathan
    Michael Gray, *Oaths and the English Reformation* (Cambridge, 2013);
    John Kerrigan, *Shakespeare's Binding Language* (Oxford, 2016).

24 R. C. Bald, *John Donne: A Life* (Oxford, 1970), pp. 123–4; Donne,
    Complete Poems, ed. Robbins, p. 423.

25 Donne, 'A Second Sermon Preached at *White-hall. April* 21. 1618',
    in *Sermons Preached at the Jacobean Courts, 1615–1619*, vol. 1, ed. Peter
    McCullough (Oxford, 2015), pp. 99–112, at pp. 110–11. See also
    John Krause, 'The Montaignicity of Donne's "Metempsychosis"',
    in Barbara Lewalski, ed., *Renaissance Genres: Essays on Theory, History and
    Interpretation* (Cambridge, MA, 1986), pp. 418–43, at pp. 419–20.

26 Joel C. Relihan, *Ancient Menippean Satire* (Baltimore, MD, 1993).

27 Donne, 'Metempsychosis', in *Complete Poems*, ed. Robbins,
    pp. 422–60, at p. 426.

28 Virgil, *The Aeneid: A New Prose Translation*, ed. David West
    (Harmondsworth, 1990), p. 3; Ovid, *Metamorphoses*, p. 29. On the
    Ovidian epic character of Donne's poem see Janel M. Mueller,
    'Donne's Epic Venture in the "Metempsychosis"', *Modern Philology*,
    70 (1972), pp. 109–37.

29 Elizabeth D. Harvey, 'The Souls of Animals: John Donne's
    Metempsychosis and Early Modern Natural History', in *Environment
    and Embodiment in Early Modern England*, ed. Mary Floyd-Wilson and
    Garrett A. Sullivan Jr (Basingstoke, 2007), pp. 55–70, at p. 67.

30 On the humoral theory see Jean-Baptiste Bonnard, 'Male and
    Female Bodies According to Ancient Greek Physicians', trans.
    Lillian E. Doherty and Violaine Sebillotte Cuchet, *Clio*, 37 (2013),
    pp. 1–18; on the great soul as Robert Cecil see M. van Wyk Smith,
    'John Donne's *Metempsychosis* (Concluded)', *Review of English Studies*,
    94 (1973), pp. 141–52.

31 See John Bellamy, *The Tudor Law of Treason: An Introduction* (London,
    1979); Rebecca Lemon, *Treason by Words: Literature, Law, and Rebellion
    in Shakespeare's England* (Ithaca, NY, 2006).

32 Eamon Duffy, *Fires of Faith: Catholic England under Mary Tudor*
    (New Haven, CT, 2009).

33 See, for example, 'Sermon 1: Preached upon the Penitentiall
    Psalmes', in *The Oxford Edition of the Sermons of John Donne: XII, Sermons
    Preached at St. Paul's Cathedral, 1626*, ed. Mary Ann Lund (Oxford,
    2017), pp. 1–19, at p. 18.

34 Krause, 'Montaignicity'.

35 Frank A. Doggett, 'Donne's Platonism', *Sewanee Review*, 42 (1934),
    pp. 274–92.

36 For a recent analysis of Catholic opposition see Peter Lake, *Bad
    Queen Bess? Libels, Secret Histories, and the Politics of Publicity in the Reign of
    Queen Elizabeth I* (Oxford, 2015).

37 For discussion of Donne's conversion see Molly Murray, 'John
    Donne and the Language of De-nomination', in *The Poetics of
    Conversion in Early Modern English Literature: Verse and Change from Donne
    to Dryden* (Cambridge, 2009), pp. 69–104.

38 See ch. 2 above.

39 Donne, *Complete Poems*, ed. Robbins, p. 424.

6 Friendship

1 'Meditation 17' in *Devotions upon Emergent Occasions*, ed. Anthony
   Raspa (Montreal, 1975), p. 86.

2 Daniel Starza Smith, *John Donne and the Conway Papers: Patronage and
   Manuscript Circulation in the Early Seventeenth Century* (Oxford, 2014),
   p. 175; Arthur F. Marotti, *John Donne, Coterie Poet* (Madison, WI, 1986).

3 On Goodere see Starza Smith, *Donne and the Conway Papers*, esp.
   pp. 196–219. As well as outlining how important Goodere and

Donne's friendship was, Starza Smith makes a compelling case
that his name should be spelled 'Goodere' not 'Goodyer', as has
been common. See also Dennis Flynn, M. Thomas Hester and
Margaret Maurer, 'Goodere at Court, 1603–1610: The Early
Jacobean Decline of a Catholic Sympathizer and Its Bearing on
Donne's Letters', *John Donne Journal*, 31 (2012), pp. 61–98; Daniel
Starza Smith, 'The Poems of Sir Henry Goodere: A Diplomatic
Edition', *John Donne Journal*, 31 (2012), pp. 99–164.

4 See *The Life and Letters of Sir Henry Wotton*, ed. Logan Pearsall Smith,
   2 vols (Oxford, 1907).

5 Kathy Eden, *Friends Hold All Things in Common: Tradition, Intellectual
   Property, and the Adages of Erasmus* (New Haven, CT, 2001); Cedric
   C. Brown, *Friendship and Its Discourses in the Seventeenth Century*
   (Oxford, 2016).

6 Ben Jonson, 'Inviting a Friend to Supper', lines 1–6, in *The Cambridge
   Edition of the Works of Ben Jonson*, ed. David Bevington, Martin Butler
   and Ian Donaldson, 7 vols (Cambridge, 2012), vol. V, pp. 166–8.

7 Martial, *The Epigrams*, trans. James Michie (repr. Harmondsworth,
   1978), 5.78 (pp. 95–7).

8 Jonson, 'My Picture Left in Scotland', in *Works*, 7, pp. 102–3.

9 Charles Nicholl, *The Reckoning: The Murder of Christopher Marlowe*
   (London, 1992), esp. pp. 133–476.

10 Ian Donaldson, *Ben Jonson: A Life* (Oxford, 2011), p. 114.

11 John Donne, *Letters to Severall Persons of Honour* (London, 1651),
   pp. 48–9; John Donne, *Selected Letters*, ed. P. M. Oliver (New York,
   2002), pp. 34–5.

12 On the significance of letters see James Daybell and Andrew
   Gordon, eds, *Cultures of Correspondence in Early Modern Britain*
   (Philadelphia, PA, 2016); on Donne's aversion to print see Richard
   B. Wollman, 'The "Press and the Fire": Print and Manuscript
   Culture in Donne's Circle', *Studies in English Literature*, 33 (1993),
   pp. 85–97. For details of one major volume of letters see *The
   Correspondence of Isaac Casaubon in England*, ed. Paul Botley and Máté
   Vince, 4 vols (Geneva, 2018), vol. 1, pp. 57–8.

13 Paul E. J. Hammer, *The Polarisation of Elizabethan Politics: The Political
   Career of Robert Devereux, 2nd Earl of Essex, 1585–1597* (Cambridge,
   1999), ch. 7.

14 Starza Smith, *Donne and the Conway Papers*, pp. 200–201.

15 John Donne, *The Complete Poems of John Donne*, ed. Robin Robbins (Harlow, 2008), pp. 95–6; R. C. Bald, *John Donne: A Life* (Oxford, 1970), esp. pp. 163–71, 294–7.

16 Jonson, 'To Sir Henry Goodyer', *Works*, 5, pp. 153–4.

17 The second epigram (86) is rather more flattering and praises Goodere for his library and choice of friends, suggesting that his good qualities stem from his knowledge, but it can also be read as a reminder of what he needs to do rather than what he actually does: Jonson, *Works*, 5, p. 154.

18 Donne, 'To Sir Henry Goodyer', lines 17–20, in *Complete Poems*, ed. Robbins, pp. 95–9.

19 John Keltridge, *Two Godlie and Learned Sermons appointed, and preached, before the Jesuites, seminaries, and other adversaries to the gospell of Christ in the Tower of London* (London, 1581), p. 145.

20 Craig Muldrew, *The Economy of Obligation: The Culture of Credit and Social Relations in Early Modern England* (Basingstoke, 1997).

21 Walton, 'Life of Sir Henry Wotton', in *Lives of Donne, Wotton, Hooker, Herbert and Sanderson*, pp. 91–52, at p. 106; Bald, *A Life*, p. 43.

22 A. J. Loomie, 'Wotton, Sir Henry', Paul E. J. Hammer, 'Cuffe, Henry', ODNB.

23 Donne, *Selected Letters*, pp. 3–8; *Life and Letters of Sir Henry Wotton*, vol. 1, pp. 306–10.

24 *Life and Letters of Sir Henry Wotton*, vol. 1, p. 308.

25 Donne, *Selected Letters*, p. 3. On Essex's meeting with Tyrone see Colm Lennon, *Sixteenth-century Ireland: The Incomplete Conquest* (Dublin, 1995), p. 298.

26 Donne, *Complete Poems*, ed. Robbins, pp. 88–90.

27 Aiden Doyle, *A History of the Irish Language: From the Norman Invasion to Independence* (Oxford, 2015), p. 15.

28 John McGurk, *The Elizabethan Conquest of Ireland: The Burdens of the 1590s Crisis* (Manchester, 1997), p. 241.

29 Donne, 'To Mr Henry Wotton' ('Sir, more than kisses'), lines 1–6, in *Complete Poems*, ed. Robbins, pp. 81–8.

30 Donne, *Selected Letters*, pp. 7–8. On reading see W. Sherman and Lisa Jardine, 'Pragmatic Readers: Knowledge Transactions and Scholarly Services in Late Elizabethan England', in *Religion, Culture and Society*

in Early Modern Britain: Essays in Honour of Patrick Collinson, ed. Anthony
Fletcher and Peter Roberts (Cambridge, 1994), pp. 102–24.

31 J.N.D. Kelly, *The Oxford Dictionary of Popes* (Oxford, 1986), pp. 206–8.

32 Dante, *Inferno*, trans. Robin Kirkpatrick (Harmondsworth, 2006),
    Canto 3, lines 58–60 (pp. 22–3).

33 See Arnold Pritchard, *Catholic Loyalism in Elizabethan England*
    (London, 1979); Michael C. Questier, *Catholicism and Community
    in Early Modern England: Politics, Aristocratic Patronage and Religion,
    c. 1550–1640* (Cambridge, 2006).

34 See ch. 2 above.

35 On patrons and friends see Richard A. McCabe, '*Ungainefull Arte*':
    Poetry, Patronage, and Print in the Early Modern Era (Oxford, 2016),
    p. 19.

36 Bald, *A Life*, p. 186.

37 Robert H. Fritze, 'Kingsmill Family'; Barbara McGovern, 'Finch
    [née Kingsmill], Anne, Countess of Winchilsea', *ODNB*.

38 Donne, *Letters to Severall Persons*, pp. 1–2. *Amadis de Gaul* is a well-
    known, extremely long romance.

39 On humour see Indira Ghose, *Shakespeare and Laughter: A Cultural
    History* (Manchester, 2008); on plague see F. P. Wilson, *The Plague
    in Shakespeare's London* (Oxford, 1963).

40 Donne, 'To the Honourable Lady the Lady Kingsmill upon the
    death of Her Husband', *Letters to Severall Persons*, pp. 7–10, at p. 10.

41 Bald, *A Life*, esp. pp. 180–84.

42 Helen Payne, 'Russell [née Harington], Lucy, Countess of
    Bedford', *ODNB*.

43 Donne, *Letters to Several Persons*, p. 23.

44 Donne, 'To the Countess of Bedford at New Year's Tide', lines
    6–15, in *Complete Poems*, ed. Robbins, pp. 665–71.

45 John Barrell, 'Editing Out: The Discourse of Patronage and
    Shakespeare's Twenty-ninth Sonnet', in *Poetry, Language and Politics*
    (Manchester, 1988), pp. 1–17.

46 See above in this chapter.

47 Donne, 'To the Countess of Bedford', lines 18–24, in *Complete
    Poems*, ed. Robbins, pp. 719–20.

48 Donne, 'To the Countess of Bedford (*begun in France, but never
    perfected*)', lines 1–2, in *Complete Poems*, ed. Robbins, pp. 721–3.

49 Strangely enough the countess did fall seriously ill in November 1612, possibly from a stroke. Some critics argue that 'A Nocturnal upon Saint Lucy's Day' was written for her (see ch. 3 above), which would make that poem 'an intensely self-centred meditation' (Donne, *Complete Poems*, ed. Robbins, p. 226) and provide a link to these verse letters.

BIBLIOGRAPHICAL ESSAY

There are a number of editions of Donne's poetry. The standard work is the Variorum Edition, ed. Gary Stringer et al. (1995–), volumes of which are appearing with increasing regularity. However, its notes are very dense and readers may prefer to use other editions. Many of the older Clarendon Press editions are also useful, for example, *Satires, Epigrams and Verse Letters*, ed. W. Milgate (Oxford, 1967), and *The Epithalamions, Anniversaries, and Epicedes*, ed. W. Milgate (Oxford, 1978). *The Complete Poems of John Donne*, ed. Robin Robbins (Harlow, 2008), has very full, useful and interesting annotation (occasionally slightly eccentric); the older Penguin edition, John Donne, *The Complete Poems*, ed. A. J. Smith (Harmondsworth, 1971), is scholarly and reader-friendly, but the annotations are sparse. The best selected Donne is that by Janel Mueller in the 21st-century Authors series (2015), which is copious, judicious and has excellent notes. Donald R. Dickson's *John Donne's Poetry* (2015), in the Norton critical editions series, is another good selection with a valuable appendix of critical essays. There is also John Donne, *Selected Poetry*, ed. John Carey (Oxford, 1996). Elegant but very dated is *The Poems of John Donne*, ed. Herbert J. C. Grierson (Oxford, 1912).

The standard edition of the sermons is being published under the general editorship of Peter McCullough, *The Oxford Edition of the Sermons of John Donne*, 13 vols (Oxford, 2013–). These are all edited by first-rate scholars and have learned and useful introductions and annotations. Not all editions are published yet so *The Sermons of John Donne*, ed. G. R. Potter and E. M. Simpson, 10 vols (Berkeley, CA, 1953–62) should be consulted. The standard edition of *Pseudo-Martyr* is edited by Anthony Raspa (Montreal, 1993), as is *Devotions upon Emergent Occasions* (Montreal,

1975); *Ignatius His Conclave* is edited by T. S. Healy (Oxford, 1969) and *Paradoxes and Problems* by Helen Peters. Also worth consulting is W. Milgate's edition of *The Epithalamions, Anniversaries and Epicedes* (Oxford, 1978), which has a good section on the elegies written for Donne. P. M. Oliver's edition of John Donne, *Selected Letters* (Manchester, 2002) is judicious and has helpful headings, and there is a modern facsimile reprint of John Donne, *Letters to Severall Persons of Honour* (New York, 1974). Neil Rhodes's edition of John Donne, *Selected Prose* (Harmondsworth, 1987; rev. 2015), has an excellent selection of work from the *Sermons, Paradoxes, Biathanatos, Devotions*, as well as the sermons and the letters. Jeanne Shami provides a stimulating analysis of their importance and relation to political developments in *John Donne and Conformity in Crisis in the Late Jacobean Pulpit* (Woodbridge, 2003). There is a long and detailed section on Donne's manuscripts in Peter Beal, *Index of English Literary Manuscripts*, vol. 1: *1475–1625* (New York, 1980), pp. 243–564. Beal comments, 'As if to compensate for the paucity of verse autographs, probably more transcripts of Donne's poems were made than of any other British poet of the 16th and 17th centuries' (p. 245).

Useful resources include Homer Carroll Combs and Zay Rusk Sullens, eds, *A Concordance to the English Poems of John Donne* (New York, 1969). The John Donne Society publishes *The John Donne Journal: Studies in the Age of Donne* (1982–). The Luminarium website has a number of useful free resources (www.luminarium.org). The Virtual Paul's Cross website (https://vpcp.chass.ncsu.edu) contains a number of interesting features, including visual and acoustic tours of St Paul's Cathedral and its surrounding areas. Most significantly there is a reconstruction of Donne's Gunpowder Day sermon, 5 November 1622 (https://vpcp.chass.ncsu.edu/listen-the-sermon). A. J. Smith's *John Donne: The Critical Heritage* (London, 1983) collects the early responses to Donne and his work. John R. Roberts's two works, *John Donne: An Annotated Bibliography of Modern Criticism, 1912–67* (Columbus, OH, 1973) and *John Donne: An Annotated Bibliography of Modern Criticism, 1968–1978* (Columbus, OH, 1982), survey more recent critical works.

The standard biography is R. C. Bald, *John Donne: A Life* (Oxford, 1970), an immense work of scholarship which has not been superseded. Edmund Gosse's *The Life and Letters of John Donne* (London, 1899) is now very dated, but contains some useful information and generous selections from Donne's poetry and prose. John Stubbs's *John Donne: The Reformed Soul* (2006) contains little that is new and is rather disappointing on the works. John Carey's critical-biographical study, *John Donne: Life, Mind and Art* (1981), is a lot more enjoyable but its outline and many of the readings should be treated with caution and read against those in other critical works. Isaak Walton's *Life of Dr John Donne*, the best early source for his biography, is readily available in, for example, Isaak Walton, *The Lives of John Donne, Sir Henry Wotton, Richard Hooker, George Herbert, Robert Sanderson* (Oxford, 1927). Paul Sellin's *So Doth, So Is Religion: John Donne and Diplomatic Contexts in the Reformed Netherlands, 1619–1620* (Columbia, MO, 1988) contains a wealth of useful biographical material, as does Daniel Starza Smith's *John Donne and the Conway Papers: Patronage and Manuscript Circulation in the Early Seventeenth Century* (Oxford, 2014), expanding our knowledge of Donne's friends and patrons. David Colclough's excellent collection, *John Donne's Professional Lives* (Woodbridge, 2003), explores Donne's various professions in terms of early modern life and culture. The significance of Donne's portraits is discussed in terms of the growth of 'citizen portraiture' in Tarnya Cooper, *Citizen Portrait: Portrait Painting and the Urban Elite of Tudor and Jacobean England and Wales* (New Haven, CT, 2012) (see also her *Searching for Shakespeare* (New Haven, CT, 2006)).

There are a number of good critical anthologies that are easily available. Achsah Guibbory, *The Cambridge Companion to John Donne* (Cambridge, 2006), is lively, wide-ranging and stimulating, with a number of useful essays on Donne's representation of women (*Returning to John Donne* (London, 2015), gathers her own important essays). Michael Schoenfeldt's *John Donne in Context* (Cambridge, 2019) contains 31 short reflections by established critics on Donne's career and is a reliable guide showing how Donne is read by scholars and critics at the time of writing; *The Oxford Handbook of John Donne*, ed. Jeanne Shami, Dennis Flynn and M. Thomas Hester (Oxford, 2011), is more heavyweight and contains some valuable contributions, but is slightly difficult to navigate. Andrew Mousley's *John Donne: Contemporary Critical Essays* (Basingstoke, 1999) is very much of its time but contains some excellent essays by Tilottama Rajan, Barbara Estrin, Richard Halpern, Stanley Fish and others.

Critical studies are numerous. Murray Roston's *The Soul of Wit: A Study of John Donne* (Oxford, 1974), a work informed by the New Criticism, is alive to Donne's wit and delight in paradox. Arthur Marotti's *John Donne,*

Coterie Poet (Madison, WI, 1986) has been influential in reading Donne in terms of a culture of manuscript circulation (see also his *Manuscript, Print, and the English Renaissance Lyric* (Ithaca, NY, 1995)). Anthony Low's *The Reinvention of Love: Poetry, Politics and Culture from Sidney to Milton* (Cambridge, 1993) studies the relationship between Donne's secular and spiritual poetry. H. L. Meakin's *John Donne's Articulations of the Feminine* (Oxford, 1998) is good on Donne's learning as well as his sometimes misogynistic representation of women; Barbara Estrin argues a case for the defence in *Laura: Uncovering Gender in Wyatt, Donne, and Marvell* (Durham, NC, 1994). Ramie Targoff's *John Donne: Body and Soul* (Chicago, IL, 2008) is an influential recent study of Donne's conception of himself. Kevin Pask and Stephen Dobranski explore Donne's significance and self-presentation as an author in *The Emergence of the English Author: Scripting the Life of the Poet in Early Modern England* (Cambridge, 1996) and *Readers and Authorship in Early Modern England* (Cambridge, 2005). Margaret Fetzer reads Donne's varied outputs in terms of speech act theory and his sense of dramatic performance in *John Donne's Performances: Sermons, Poems, Letters and Devotions* (Manchester, 2010). Peter De Sa Wiggins argues that Donne was much inspired by reading manuals of courtly behaviour in *Donne, Castiglione, and the Poetry of Courtliness* (Bloomington, IN, 2000).

Some older studies are worth consulting. T. S. Eliot's essay 'The Metaphysical Poets', which argued that thought and feeling were united in Donne's poetry before there was a 'disassociation of sensibility' later in the seventeenth century, helped establish a change in taste which placed great value on Donne's vigour, honesty and love of paradox: 'The Metaphysical Poets', *Selected Essays* [1921] (London, 1951). There are some profound insights in William Empson's reading of 'A Valediction: Of Weeping' in *Seven Types of Ambiguity* (London, 1930), which also helped to establish Donne as a significant poet in the twentieth century; the brief comments on 'The Canonization' in *Some Versions of the Pastoral* (London, 1935) are also worth reading. Donne's place as a canonical poet was cemented by Cleanth Brooks in his reading of the same poem in his *The Well-wrought Urn: Studies in the Structure of Poetry* (New York, 1947). Taking its title from Donne, this seminal New Critical study of Donne cast him as one of the most profound poets of studied ambiguity. H.J.C. Grierson's and Helen Gardner's anthologies, *Metaphysical Lyrics and Poems of the Seventeenth Century* (Oxford, 1921) and *The Metaphysical Poets* (Harmondsworth,

1957), are valuable for the ways in which they show why Donne became such a significant poet and how he was read; there is a revised edition of Gardner's anthology edited by Colin Burrow (2006). Other older studies are worth consulting: J. B. Leishman's *The Monarch of Wit: An Analytical and Comparative Study of the Poetry of John Donne* (London, 1951) contains astute critical judgements; James Winny's *A Preface to Donne* (London, 1970) is dated, but has some lively insights, is well-conceived as an introduction and has interesting and useful illustrations and pictures. A. J. Smith's *Donne: Songs and Sonnets* (London, 1964) is also dated, but has the insights of a life-long study of Donne. There are two essays on Donne in *Elizabethan and Jacobean Studies Presented to Frank Percy Wilson* (Oxford, 1959): Kathleen Tillotson on Donne's poor reputation in the nineteenth century and Helen Gardner's defence of Donne as a major poet, centred on a reading of 'The Ecstasy' as a serious work of Neoplatonism. Rosamund Tuve's influential *Elizabethan and Metaphysical Imagery: Renaissance Poetry and Twentieth-century Critics* (Chicago, IL, 1947) is not to be trusted on the tone and style of Donne's poetry, but explains a great deal about the culture of shared images out of which his writing developed.

Some of the best recent work on Donne has concentrated on his theology and relationship to patristic learning, as well as his confessional allegiance and understanding of the Christian Church. Not all scholars and critics agree about Donne's religious orientation. John Stachniewski in *The Persecutory Imagination: English Puritanism and the Literature of Religious Despair* (Oxford, 1991) argues for a Calvinist-inspired Donne; Dennis Flynn in *John Donne and the Ancient Catholic Nobility* (Bloomington, IN, 1995), for a Catholic one. Debora Kuller Shuger's *Habits of Thought in the English Renaissance: Religion, Politics and the Dominant Culture* (Toronto, 1997) sees Donne as a believer in 'absolutist theology', regarding the monarch as God's sacred representative on earth. The study by Katrin Ettenhuber, *Donne's Augustine: Renaissance Cultures of Interpretation* (Oxford, 2011), is exemplary, as are the readings and contextualizations of the religious poems by Brian Cummings in *The Literary Culture of the Reformation: Grammar and Grace* (Oxford, 2002). Molly Murray argues that Donne had an unusually positive and open sense of conversion in *The Poetics of Conversion in Early Modern English Literature: Verse and Change from Donne to Dryden* (Cambridge, 2009). Susannah Brietz Monta is equally perceptive on Donne in her study, *Martyrdom and Literature in Early Modern England* (Cambridge, 2005).

Hannibal Hamlin shows how Donne's poetry is informed by his reading of the psalms in *Psalm Culture and Early Modern English Literature* (Cambridge, 2004); Noam Flinker does the same for 'The Song of Songs' in *The Song of Songs in English Renaissance Literature* (Woodbridge, 2000); and Mary Morrissey's *Politics and the Paul's Cross Sermons, 1558–1642* (Oxford, 2011) explores the Reformation context in which Donne preached. David Wootton has an unusual approach to Donne's religion in John Brooke and Ian Maclean, eds, *Heterodoxy in Early Modern Science and Religion* (Oxford, 2005), which is a salutary reminder of what people might have believed in times of religious strife and why.

Important discussions of other aspects of Donne's wide-ranging interests and accomplishments can be found in a number of studies. Diane Kelsey McColley reveals the importance of music in Donne's poetry in *Poetry and Music in Seventeenth-century England* (Cambridge, 1997); Jonathan Sawday explores Donne's representation of the body in *The Body Emblazoned: Dissection and the Human Body in Renaissance Culture* (London, 1995). Eric Langley's *Narcissism and Suicide in Shakespeare and His Contemporaries* (2009) has some astute critical reflections on *Biathanatos*, as does Brian Cummings's *Mortal Thoughts: Religion, Secularity and Identity in Shakespeare and Early Modern Culture* (Oxford, 2013). Gregory Kneidel reads the satires to show how knowledgeable Donne was about law and legal practices in *John Donne and Early Modern Legal Culture: The End of Equity in the Satyres* (Pittsburgh, PA, 2015), and the essay by Emma Rhatigan in Jayne Elisabeth Archer, Elizabeth Goldring and Sarah Knight's collection, *The Intellectual and Cultural World of the Early Modern Inns of Court* (Manchester, 2011), provides an overview of Donne preaching at the Inns of Court. Lawrence Manley is thorough and insightful on Donne as a London writer in *Literature and Culture in Early Modern London* (Cambridge, 1995). Katrin Ettenhuber's essay on Donne and grief in Brian Cummings and Freya Sierhuis's collection, *Passions and Subjectivity in Early Modern Culture* (Abingdon, 2013), is also valuable. Ian Frederick Moulton explains the culture of erotic manuscript verse in which Donne participated in *Before Pornography: Erotic Writing in Early Modern England* (Oxford, 2000).

ACKNOWLEDGEMENTS

My special thanks to Shanyn Altman, with whom I have worked on Donne for many years and who read the complete typescript, making numerous suggestions and saving me from some egregious errors. Also to Peter Boxall, Neil Rhodes and James Shapiro, who were equally self-sacrificing and helpful in reading the whole work. My thanks also to Nick Royle, who supplied me with the Derrida reference. It has been a pleasure to work with Reaktion Books; in particular with Michael Leaman and François Quiviger, who read the manuscript and made many helpful suggestions, with Martha Jay, and with Alex Ciobanu, who has gone well beyond the call of duty in hunting out images.

PHOTO ACKNOWLEDGEMENTS

The author and publishers wish to express their thanks to the below sources of illustrative material and/or permission to reproduce it. Some locations of artworks are also given below, in the interest of brevity:

Biblioteca Nacional do Brasil, Rio de Janeiro: p. 95; British Library, London (Add MS 71474): p. 34; Cappella di San Brizio, Duomo di Orvieto: p. 62; Christ Church Picture Gallery, Oxford/photo reproduced by permission of the Governing Body of Christ Church, Oxford (LP 69): p. 136; from John Donne, *Deaths Duell; or, A Consolation to the Soule, against the dying Life, and living Death of the Body* (London, 1632): p. 33; from John Donne, *Poems, by J. D. With Elegies on the Authors Death* (London, 1633): pp. 176, 177; from John Donne, *Poems, by J. D. With Elegies on the Authors Death*, 4th edn, 3rd issue (London, 1654): p. 17; photo Paul Dykes, reproduced with permission: p. 39; Foreign and Commonwealth Office, Whitehall, London: p. 189; Gemäldegalerie Alte Meister, Dresden: p. 90; Library of Congress, Prints and Photographs Division, Washington, DC: pp. 150–51; Museo Civico di Castel Nuovo, Naples: p. 197; Museo de Bellas Artes de Sevilla: p. 38; Museo del Prado, Madrid: p. 162; The National Gallery, London: p. 80; National Gallery of Art, Washington, DC: p. 41; National Portrait Gallery, London: pp. 14, 94, 167, 179; Nationalmuseum, Stockholm/photo Linn Ahlgren: p. 82; private collection: p. 200; Royal Collection Trust/© Her Majesty Queen Elizabeth II 2021: p. 46; Society of Antiquaries of London: p. 50; from Thomas Speight, ed., *The Workes of our Ancient and learned English Poet, Geoffrey Chaucer, newly Printed* (London, 1602): p. 159; Victoria and Albert Museum, London: p. 6.

INDEX

Illustration numbers are indicated by *italics*.